AN

INVESTIGATION

OF THE

TRINITY OF PLATO

AND OF

PHILO JUDÆUS.

Βέλτιον ἴσως ἐπισκέψασθαι, καὶ διαπορῆσαι, πῶς λέγεται, καίπερ προσάντους τῆς τοιαύτης γενομένης ζητήσεως, διὰ τὸ φίλους ἄνδρας εἰσαγαγεῖν τὰ εἴδη. δόξειε δ' ἂν ἴσως βέλτιον εἶναι, καὶ δεῖν ἐπὶ σωτηρίᾳ γε τῆς ἀληθείας, καὶ τὰ οἰκεῖα ἀναιρεῖν, ἄλλως τε καὶ φιλοσόφους ὄντας· ἀμφοῖν γὰρ ὄντοιν φίλοιν, ὅσιον προτιμᾶν τὴν ἀλήθειαν.

ARISTOT. *Ethic. Nicom.* Lib. I. Cap. iv.

AN INVESTIGATION

OF THE

TRINITY OF PLATO

AND OF

PHILO JUDÆUS

AND OF THE EFFECTS WHICH AN ATTACHMENT TO THEIR WRITINGS
HAD UPON THE PRINCIPLES AND REASONINGS OF THE
FATHERS OF THE CHRISTIAN CHURCH

BY

CÆSAR MORGAN, D.D.
CHAPLAIN TO THE LORD BISHOP OF ELY

Edited for the Syndics of the University Press

PUBLISHERS
Eugene, Oregon

Wipf and Stock Publishers
199 W 8th Ave, Suite 3
Eugene, OR 97401

An Investigation of the Trinity of Plato and of Philo Judaeus
And of the effects which an attachment to their writings had
upon the principles and reasonings of the Fathers of the Christian church
By Morgan, Caesar
ISBN: 1-59752-221-X
Publication date 5/25/2005
Previously published by Cambridge, 1853

Advertisement to the Present Edition.

CÆSAR MORGAN, the Author of the following work, was educated at the Grammar School of Haverfordwest, and at Christ's College, Cambridge, where he was admitted a scholar in the year 1769. He took the degree of B.A. in 1773, that of M.A. in 1776, and that of D.D. in 1793. In the year 1775 he was elected to a Fellowship of his College, which he vacated by marriage in 1776, the year in which his tutor, Archdeacon PALEY, ceased to be a member of that Foundation.

He subsequently became Chaplain to Bishop YORKE, by whom he was presented to the Vicarage of Littleport and to a stall in the Church of Ely in 1804, having been previously a minor canon in the same Cathedral.

In 1785 Mr MORGAN obtained the honorary prize given by TEYLER's Theological Society at Haarlem for an essay, of which the following is the title, A demonstration that true philosophy has no tendency to undermine divine revelation, and that a well-grounded philosopher may be a true Christian[*]. The essay was originally printed at Haarlem in 1786, subsequently at the Cambridge University Press in 1787. In 1795 DR MORGAN published his 'Investigation of the Trinity

---
[*] See note, page 164.

of Plato and of Philo Judæus, etc.' *a treatise which probably attracted much attention at the time of its publication: but is now very little known, although it forms a most valuable, indeed necessary, supplement to the writings of Bull, Allix and Horsley on the same subject. The republication of the work will, it is hoped, procure for it a wider circulation than it has hitherto found.*

The present edition has been carefully revised, the references of the quotations have been verified and completed, (all additional matter being enclosed between brackets), and a synoptical Table of Contents has been prefixed. The paging of the original Edition is noted in the margin.

H. A. HOLDEN.

TRINITY COLLEGE,
1853, *February* 5.

TO

THE HONOURABLE AND RIGHT REVEREND

JAMES,

LORD BISHOP OF ELY.

My Lord,

The work which I have now the honour of addressing to your Lordship, though begun, and in a great measure executed, under the pressure of bodily infirmity and amidst numerous daily avocations, has been often carefully reviewed by me at leisure. For this leisure, I am proud thus publicly to acknowledge that I am indebted solely to your Lordship's unsolicited patronage. It has been sometimes a subject of debate among nice observers of human nature, whether a relaxation from business and an encrease of income bring with them those means of real enjoyment, which men fondly expect from them. But of this there can be no doubt, that it is a great consolation to the weary spirit not to be obliged to toil when the strength faileth. Whatever, therefore, shall be my future designation in this life;

> Seu me tranquilla senectus
> Expectat; seu mors atris circumvolat alis;
> Dives, inops, Romæ, seu sors ita jusserit, exul;
> Quisquis erit vitæ color;

As long as I support this 'frail and feverish being;' I shall ever retain the warmest sense of the favours conferred upon,

My Lord,

Your Lordship's

Most grateful and devoted
Servant and Chaplain,

CÆSAR MORGAN.

SYNOPSIS OF CONTENTS.

INTRODUCTION. Value of acquaintance with the writings of ancient philosophers, particularly those of Plato: his acquaintance with the doctrine of the Trinity of persons in the Divine nature, heretofore not doubted: passage in the *Philebus* misconstrued by Cudworth: doctrines of Plato generally misapprehended by the Fathers of the Christian Church: hence necessity for original examination of his writings: Ammonius, Plotinus, Cudworth, Le Clerc: 'plan pursued by the Author: anecdote: Mosheim differs from Cudworth in his interpretation of Plato .... p. i

Plato's *Epinomis*, passage in examined and meaning of the word λόγος deduced: doctrine of the Dialogue, what ....p. 1

The *Parmenides*, difficulty of, arising from its being so *abstracted*: variety of opinions about, Serranus, Le Clerc: Cudworth follows Plotinus: peculiarity of the Dialogue in relation to Socrates: examination of it: subject of the debate: illustrated from the *Philebus*: from the *Republic*, Book v: Aristotle's exception to the reasoning of Melissus and Parmenides ... p. 8

Plato's *Doctrine of Ideas*: Aristotle's doctrine on the same: division of knowledge into two kinds in the *Philebus* ....p. 23

Determination of the meaning of τὸ ἀγαθόν in Plato: mistake of Plotinus, Cudworth: the question concerning the greatest good considered of the highest importance by all sects of heathen philosophers: Cicero: Socrates, his exposition of it in Plato, in Xenophon: Aristotle's conclusion that there is not a common good, directed against Plato's theory: Τὸ ἀγαθόν never intended by Plato to express a *person* ....p. 27

The *Philebus*: misinterpretation of passage in (νοῦς ἐστὶ γενούσης τοῦ πάντων αἰτίου): _Context of it examined: Platonic doctrine, that the soul of man is akin to and derived from the soul of the Universe, supported by quotations from Cicero and Maximus Tyrius .... p. 36

Plato's Epistles .... p. 43

The *Cratylus*—passage in, examined .... p. 47

The *Timæus*—subject of investigated: derived from the Treatise of Timæus the Locrian, concerning the Soul of the world: meaning of terms employed in: Plato's opinion concerning the Eternity of the world: doctrine of Pythagoras, of the Stoics: hypothesis of Plato's acquaintance with the doctrine of three *hypostases* in the Divine nature not countenanced by any of the above passages .... p. 48

This doctrine not attributed to him by the subsequent philosophers of Greece or Rome .... p. 61

Philo Judæus the cause of its being so attributed: conformity between his principles and those of Plato proved against the assertion of Allix: his use of the term λόγος θεῖος: design of Philo's writings overlooked by his interpreters: his use of κοσμὸς νοητός: of λόγος .... p. 63

Allegorical method of interpreting Scripture was derived from Philo: notion that the philosophical principles of Pagan antiquity were directly or indirectly derived from Scripture, common to Jewish and Christian writers of old, e.g. Josephus, Justin Martyr, Clemens Alexandrinus: Origen: Philo's allegorical method in high estimation among the Fathers, Clemens and Theophilus: effect of these two circumstances on the reasonings of the Christians of the second century traced in Justin Martyr, Athenagoras, Theophilus, Tertullian: error of Praxeas: orthodox writers and heretics of the second century agreed in their original general principles, but differed in their application of them: illustration of this from a passage of Tertullian concerning the system of Valentinus: Gnostics, their doctrines said by Irenæus to be primarily derived from the philosophy of Plato: testimony of Clemens Alexandrinus to the same effect: of Plotinus: Gnostic heresies wrongly supposed to owe their origin to the Oriental Philosophy alone: true statement of the case: establishment of the school of Ammonius Saccas at Alexandria: important effect of on Christianity: frequent endeavours on the part of Christian writers to make out a conformity between their own profession and heathen tradition, not responded to by the Pagan philosophers till this time, when they began to proclaim that there was nothing new in Christianity: Plotinus, his writings: the principal doctrine which he endeavours to prove by abstract reasoning, and to support by Plato's authority, is a Trinity in the Divine nature: quotations from: allegorical mode of interpreting Pagan mythology assailed by Arnobius: Origen an admirer of Philo's system: heresy of Sabellius, refuted by Dionysius, bishop of Alexandria, who was defended by Athanasius because the Arians tried to shelter themselves under his authority: controversy between Arius and Alexander to be understood by a reference to the sophisticated doctrines of Philo..p. 120

CONCLUSION .... p. 149

LIST OF EDITIONS USED BY THE AUTHOR.

ATHANASIUS	Paris. 1627
ATHENAGORAS	Paris. 1636 fo.
CLEMENS ALEXANDRINUS	Paris. 1640
CUDWORTH'S *Intellectual System*	London 1673
IRENÆUS	Paris. 1639
JUSTIN MARTYR	Paris. 1636
ORIGENES	Huet. *Roth.* 1668
ORIGENES contra Celsum.	Spencer. *Cant.* 1677
PHILO JUDÆUS	Turneb. et Hœschel. *Paris.*1640
PLATO	Serranus, *Paris.* 1578
PLOTINUS	*Basileæ* 1580
TERTULLIANUS	Pamelius, *Paris.* 1608

INTRODUCTION.

ALL the works of God are wonderful in their kind and display, in either a minute or stupendous manner, the wisdom and benevolence of the Creator. Philosophy, in its several branches, initiates men into the great mysteries of the creation, and, by unfolding the principles, upon which it was at first conducted and is still supported, leads us to admire, to reverence, and adore the author of all things. It is for this reason the most valuable gift, that by the ordinary course of nature has been bestowed upon man.

There is nothing in the whole order of existence, upon which the supreme Being has not impressed unequivocal marks of himself; and therefore nothing in nature is so insignificant, or so far removed from us (provided it can be subjected to the notice of our understanding or our senses) that the contemplation of it will not be highly gratifying to a rational mind, and useful for some of the various purposes of human life. But, as intellectual and moral beings assert an undisputed claim to the first place in the scale of nature, and approach nearest in rank and excellence to the Deity; the contemplation of the mind itself, the source of that distinction and superiority over other less favoured animals of its powers and defects, and of the best methods of extending the one and correcting the other, must be the most noble, the most exalted, and at the same time the most useful exercise of the human intellect.

On this account I have ever set a high value upon the knowledge of pagan antiquity, particularly upon an acquaintance with the writings of the philosophers of ancient Greece. In them we see the human understanding in its natural and unassisted state, putting forth its most vigorous and best directed exertions in the pursuit of truth; and we may thence learn to set a just value upon that communication of wisdom, so pure, so simple, and so unadorned, which is tendered to us in the Gospel of Christ.

But, besides this general advantage which attends the study of all the philosophic writings of ancient Greece, that have escaped the wreck of time; the writings of PLATO stand eminently distinguished by a privilege almost peculiarly their own. They were for some ages the principal study of the Fathers of the Christian Church; and the doctrines which I have undertaken particularly to discuss, were, by their fond partiality, in a manner incorporated into the system of Christianity. By a strange fatality, all sects of religion, however they differed from each other in the conclusions which they deduced from it, agreed in this opinion, that the great and distinguishing doctrines of Christianity were to be found in the writings of PLATO. Nor is that opinion abandoned by the generality of the Christians of the present day, who recur to the writings of the early defenders of our faith, for a knowledge of the doctrines maintained by the Church in those primitive times.

The course of my own reading had led me to adopt the commonly received opinion, that PLATO had some knowledge of the profound and mystical doctrine of the Trinity. I was the less inclined to question the truth of this opinion, as it was almost the only one in which the controversialists of the present day were generally agreed. When, therefore, I was excited to enter into a minute examination of this subject, my original object was not to ascertain the truth of the opinion, that PLATO was acquainted with the doctrine of the Trinity of persons in the divine nature. Of this I entertained no doubt. But I wished to know by what authority, or by what train of reasoning, he was led to embrace this doctrine; by what arguments he supported it; and in what sense he explained it. So far was I from entertaining prejudices in favour of the side of the question, which I have since found reason to maintain, that I did not even suspect the possibility of its being true, at the time when I instituted the inquiry.

When I first read the *Philebus*, I was much more disposed to distrust my own understanding, than to believe that CUDWORTH could possibly have been guilty of so glaring a mistake in the meaning of the passage, ὅτι νοῦς ἐστὶ γενούστης τοῦ πάντων αἰτίου. I read over the passage many times, and considered it with the most intense exertion of thought; nor could I prevail upon myself to adopt my own interpretation of it, till I was clearly convinced by repeated examinations, that it could not admit of any other.

[Plato *Phileb.* p. 30. E.]

When I discovered that the doctrine could derive no countenance from this passage, I still supposed that I should find it clearly proved in others. But the same disappointment still attended me in my inquiries. The farther I proceeded, the more I was persuaded, that the abstract doctrines of PLATO are at present but little understood: that false notions of them were gradually introduced among the early Fathers of the Christian Church, in a great measure by mistaken interpretations of the writings of PHILO JUDÆUS: and that those erroneous opinions were extended and formed into a system by AMMONIUS SACCAS. The most essential parts of this system have, by the authority of him and his immediate followers, been almost implicitly embraced ever since.

It may perhaps be thought a proof of great presumption, to undertake to oppose the concurrent voice of the best and wisest men for so many ages. But when it is recolleted, how many errors of antiquity have been confuted since the revival of literature and the introduction of sound philosophy into this kingdom, some will, I trust, be disposed to pay a candid and unprejudiced attention to the reasonings which I shall produce in the following Treatise, and will pass an impartial sentence, according as they shall be influenced by the preponderating evidence.

The writings of the Fathers abound with many fanciful and mystical interpretations of the Holy Scriptures themselves, which the sober criticism of the present age would hardly be prevailed upon to admit. If, therefore, we submit not implicitly to their authority in matters which fell more regularly within their province; why should we think them infallible upon subjects which were more remote from their immediate department, and more obscure and abstracted in their own nature?

To urge in their favour that they lived nearer the time of PLATO than we do, by many hundred years, is a mere fallacy. They were too far removed from him to derive any authority from that presumption. Even at their time and in their circumstances, the best and only satisfactory method of arriving at a correct knowledge of the opinions of PLATO, was by a careful perusal of those writings in which they are maintained.

This source is open to us as well as to them. To those writings I appeal, and shall endeavour to extract their genuine sense by a careful attention to the context, to the chain of argument which the author is carrying on, and to the point which he is endeavouring to establish. If any ambiguities still remain, I shall endeavour to clear them up by recurring to other dialogues of the same author, where the same terms are used, the same topics explained, and the same arguments enforced in a more simple or more perspicuous manner. This I have ever considered as the most certain and only rational method of arriving at the genuine meaning of any author, sacred or profane.

I shall produce in support of many of my interpretations, pointed, and, as I think, decisive passages from other ancient authors. I do not know that my general doctrine is in one instance contradicted by the testimony or reasoning of any pagan writer, from the time of PLATO to the latter end of the second, or the beginning of the third century of the Christian æra, when the Lectures of AMMONIUS, and the writings of his scholar

PLOTINUS, gave a new turn to the heathen philosophy. The sages who lived in the intermediate time, however distinguished they may have been by their genius and industry, and how much soever they may have reverenced and imitated PLATO, had not sagacity enough to make those discoveries which were reserved for the sophists of Alexandria. They, in the decline of all other branches of learning, were able to explore the dark recesses of the Platonic philosophy, and to point out in it, and develope mysterious doctrines, which had escaped the penetration of Greece and Rome, when they were supposed to have cultivated philosophy and the arts with the greatest celebrity and success.

In the course of my inquiry, I shall be under the necessity of differing very widely from Dr CUDWORTH, whose authority is deservedly held to be of the greatest weight in all speculations of this kind, when there is nothing but man's authority to which we can appeal. But when the case is capable of being examined and determined by legitimate reasoning, that decision is superior to all human authority. At a time when these kingdoms were distracted by contending parties in Church and State, Dr CUDWORTH must have been closely employed in laying up that fund of knowledge, from which he afterwards so copiously drew his materials, while he was composing his *True Intellectual System of the Universe.* In that work he has repelled the assaults of Atheism, and defended the principles of natural religion with astonishing skill and erudition. But, by resigning himself too implicitly to the guidance of PLOTINUS and PROCLUS, he has given his sanction to opinions, which in earlier times embarrassed the reasonings of the orthodox, and diffused a specious air of consistency over the doctrines of heretics.

While I detect a few inadvertencies in the writings of this great man, which are the more dangerous on account of his general excellencies, I never for a moment forget, or cease to reverence, his superior attainments; and I always rejoice that his destination in life was conformable to his favourite pursuits, which is almost the consummation of the earthly happiness of a literary man. For, next to his intellectual endowments, it was the peculiar felicity and distinguishing honour of CUDWORTH, to be placed at the head of a great literary society*, at a time when it was highly renowned for having recently produced MEDE and MILTON, both eminent for their various learning, and the one as profound a Divine, the other as sublime a Poet, as the world ever saw.

* Fuller, in his *History of the University of Cambridge,* which was published in the early part of the mastership of Dr Cudworth, speaks of Christ College in the following terms:

I conceive that what I have said about differing in opinion from CUDWORTH will justify me in not submitting implicitly to the authority of LE CLERC, and other ingenious men, whose names are, with the greatest reason, in the highest esteem, and whose learning, abilities, and laborious exertions, have contributed much to the support, illustration, and advancement of rational religion and genuine Christianity.

When a train of reasoning appears to any mind to be founded upon solid and incontrovertible principles: when each succeeding step of the argument is apprehended to arise necessarily out of that which preceded it, and the conclusion seems to be a clear and satisfactory deduction from the whole; I do not see what room there can be for the interposition of any human authority. While the mind is so circumstanced, it cannot submit to the authority without renouncing its reason. However modest a man possessed of such a mind may be; however diffident of his own powers; how much soever he may be disposed to submit to the opinions of others upon proper occasions; he cannot, in this instance, listen to the voice of authority, till he shall be con-

'It may without flattery be said of this house, *Many daughters have done virtuously, but thou excellest them all;* if we consider the many divines, who in so short a time have here had their education,' p. 91.

vinced that his principles are uncertain, or his deductions fallacious. Nor is he unreasonable in requesting those who undertake to accompany him in the investigation, to confine their attention entirely to those essential points which exclude the consideration of all foreign and adventitious circumstances, till they are invalidated.

When I seriously entertained the thought of laying my sentiments before the public, I was impressed with so strong a sense of the dignity of the subject, that I thought myself bound in duty to lay by the produce of my labours till the warmth of inquiry had subsided: to review it repeatedly at distant intervals: and to peruse, with the strictest attention, what had been advanced by others that seemed to bear any relation to the subject.

It would have been a much more easy task to me to have been diffuse, and seemingly more elaborate, in exhibiting as well my own opinions as those of others. But I have taken some pains to be as brief in my expositions as was consistent with order and perspicuity.

It would answer no useful purpose to combat all the systems which appear to me to be erroneous; or to invalidate the many arguments that may seem to bear some weight against the opinions which I have advanced. I thought it would best answer the purpose that I had in view if I confined myself chiefly to a simple exposition of the genuine meaning of the passages which are usually produced in defence of the opposite doctrine, and of the principal reasons that induced me to adopt the interpretation which I have exhibited.

I therefore request that no reader will, from a slight and superficial view of the subject, and under the influence of a few popular positions and obvious objections, hastily condemn, in a summary manner, what I have here laid down; but will give me credit for having bestowed much consideration upon the arguments usually advanced on the other side of the question, and for having satisfied myself after deep reflection, of the insufficiency of them to maintain the cause, for the support of which they were produced.

To induce him the more readily to grant me this indulgence, I will take the liberty of reciting to him a well-authenticated story. When the present authorized translation of the Old and New Testament came out under the auspices of King JAMES, that great work did not escape critical censures. It happened that one of the translators, soon after the completion of that arduous undertaking, made a visit to a friend in a part of the country where he was not generally known. On the Sunday he accompanied his friend to the parish church, where the officiating clergyman, in the course of his sermon took an opportunity of depreciating the new translation in general terms, and in particular assigned five reasons why a certain passage ought to have been differently translated. As the preacher dined that day with the gentleman, the translator did not omit to advert in private to the discourse that had been publicly delivered. Among other things, *quæ dicenda forent*, he told the preacher that those five reasons which he so pompously displayed in the pulpit had been all considered and deliberately weighed by the translators; but that thirteen more forcible reasons had constrained them to render the passage in the manner in which it stood in the present translation.

I am not insensible to the great weight of opposing authorities. I have, however, the satisfaction to find that I do not stand quite alone in many of my opinions. The very learned and judicious MOSHEIM has taken frequent opportunities of condemning the subtilties of the later Platonists.

[Hom. *Iliad.* X. 242.]
Εἰ μὲν δὴ ἕταρόν γε κελεύετέ μ' αὐτὸν ἑλέσθαι,
Πῶς ἂν ἔπειτ' Ὀδυσῆος ἐγὼ θείοιο λαθοίμην,
Οὗ πέρι μὲν πρόφρων κραδίη καὶ θυμὸς ἀγήνωρ
Ἐν πάντεσσι πόνοισι, φιλεῖ δὲ ἑ Παλλὰς Ἀθήνη;

In those valuable notes which accompany his Latin Version of CUDWORTH he often expresses his dissent from his author's interpretations of PLATO and PHILO; though the nature and extent of his undertaking did not require that he should always enter into a minute examination of the precise meaning of the passages in question*.

xvi In my investigation of the opinions of the Fathers of the Christian Church, I acted exactly in the same manner as I did when I examined the writings of PLATO and PHILO, as far as concerned the doctrines which they taught, and the meaning of the passages in which those doctrines were expressed. When they quoted the writings of other authors, whether sacred or profane, in defence of their tenets, I took the same liberty with them which I have always thought myself not only authorized, but bound to take in matters of such high import with every other uninspired writer. I examined with all possible care and attention the fidelity and accuracy of the quotation, the justness of the exposition, and the force of the application and deduction. If I seemed to myself to detect errors in any of those particulars, the respect which I entertained for the venerable authors on account of their industry, learning, and piety, did not suffer me to judge of them lightly or rashly. No fondness for novelty, no pleasure in discovering the defects

---

* Nimis mihi longa, eaque huic instituto parum conducens ingredienda esset disputatio, si totam explicare vellem et explanare Platonis augmentationem.—MOSHEIM. *Observ. ad* Pag. 627. Tom. I.

of others influenced my judgment. Genuine truth was the only object of my inquiry; and indeed I was conscious that nothing but truth could bear me up against such great, such long-established, and such accumulated authority.

When I endeavoured, with all the candour that I was capable of exercising, to trace their errors and false reasonings to their source, I thought I saw them originate from an ardent zeal for the advancement of the great cause which they had undertaken, the cause of GOD and of his CHRIST. This led them, without due consideration, to embrace the opinion that the doctrine of a Trinity of Persons in the Divine Nature is taught in the writings of PLATO and PHILO JUDÆUS; an opinion, according to my conception, so remote from the truth, that nothing but error can be founded upon it. With an examination of this opinion, I shall begin the investigation.

EPINOMIS.

THE following passage in the *Epinomis* is sup- [p.986. c.] posed by [1]some to establish Plato's belief of the creation of the world by the Logos, the second person of the Holy Trinity: ξυναποτελῶν κόσμον, ὃν ἔταξε λόγος ὁ πάντων θειότατος ὁρατόν. Before the design and general reasoning of the Dialogue be considered, it will be proper to observe, that a strong tincture of Pythagorean principles is conspicuous in many of the Dialogues of Plato, but in none more than in the Dialogue now under contemplation.

The *Epinomis* is to be understood to be a continuation of the dialogue Περὶ Νομοθεσίας, and is carried on by the same characters. This cir-
2 cumstance, as well as the subject of their future inquiry, is stated very clearly by Clineas[2] in the beginning. The Athenian, who undertook to discuss the subject, having touched upon the necessary, the ornamental, and the useful arts, concludes, that the knowledge of none of them will

[1] Vide Clerici *Epist. Critic.* VII. p. 241. *Amst.* 1700, and Bruckeri *Hist. Crit. Philosoph.* Pars II. Lib. ii. cap. 6, § 1, p. 692.

[2] Τὰ μὲν γὰρ ἄλλα, ὥς φαμεν, ἅπαντα διεξήλθομεν, ὅσα ἦν περὶ νόμων θέσιν· ὁ δὲ μέγιστον εὑρεῖν τε καὶ εἰπεῖν, τί ποτε μαθὼν θνητὸς ἄνθρωπος σοφὸς ἂν εἴη, τοῦτο οὔτε εἴπομεν, οὔτε εὕρομεν. νῦν δὲ πειρώμεθα τοῦτο μὴ καταλιπεῖν. [p. 973. A,B.]

intitle any one to the name of a wise man. He then proceeds to inquire, what knowledge that is, the want of which would render man the most irrational of animals. This, he says, is the knowledge of number, which he considers as the gift of some god to man. For it would be absurd to suppose, that the author of all other good things to us should not be the author of the greatest also, which is Wisdom. Without the knowledge of number a man cannot have reason (λόγος³ ;) if he were destitute of sound reason, he would not be wise, if he should not attain wisdom, which is a 3 very considerable ingredient in all virtue, he would not be completely good or happy.

The God, that gave number, is the heaven, who taught men the first principles of numera-

³ Στερόμενος δὲ ἀληθοῦς λόγου, σοφὸς οὐκ ἄν ποτε γένοιτο· ὅτῳ δὲ σοφία μὴ προσείη, πάσης ἀρετῆς τὸ μέγιστον μέρος, οὐκ ἂν ἔτι τελέως ἀγαθὸς γενόμενος, εὐδαίμων ποτε γένοιτο· οὕτως ἀριθμὸν μὲν ἀνάγκη πᾶσα ὑποτίθεσθαι. [p. 977 D.] This doctrine is similar to what he says in his *Republic*, (Lib. vii. p. 522.) τὸ ἕν τε καὶ τὰ δύο καὶ τὰ τρία διαγιγνώσκειν. Λέγω δὲ αὐτὸ ὡς ἐν κεφαλαίῳ ἀριθμόν τε καὶ λογισμόν· ἢ οὐχ οὕτω περὶ τούτων ἔχει, ὡς πᾶσα τέχνη τε καὶ ἐπιστήμη ἀναγκάζεται αὐτῶν μέτοχος γίγνεσθαι; and in the *Philebus*: Πασῶν που τεχνῶν ἄν τις ἀριθμητικὴν χωρίζῃ, καὶ μετρητικὴν, καὶ στατικὴν, ὡς ἔπος εἰπεῖν, φαῦλον τὸ καταλειπόμενον ἑκάστης ἂν γίγνοιτο. [p: 55 E.]

⁴ The same method of instructing men in number is likewise mentioned in the *Timœus*, p. 39[B]: Ἥλιον· ἵνα ὅτι μάλιστα εἰς ἅπαντα φαίνοι τὸν οὐρανόν, μετάσχοι τε ἀριθμοῦ τὰ ζῶα, ὅσοις ἦν προσῆκον, μαθόντα παρὰ τῆς ταὐτοῦ καὶ ὁμοίου περιφορᾶς. Philo also, adopting the same doctrine, says, the stars were placed in heaven to answer many purposes—Πολλῶν χάριν—ἡμερῶν, μηνῶν, ἐνιαυτῶν, ἃ δὴ καὶ μέτρα γέγονε—εὐθύς τε τὸ χρησιμώτατον, ἡ ἀριθμοῦ φύσις ἐδείχθη, χρόνου παραφήναντος αὐτήν· ἐκ γὰρ μιᾶς ἡμέρας τὸ ἕν, καὶ ἐκ δυοῖν τὰ δύο, καὶ ἐκ τριῶν τὰ τρία. Περὶ Κοσμοποιίας: pag. 11, 12.

EPINOMIS. 3

tion by the [4]succession of day and night, the variations of the moon, &c. He likewise taught them, what is more important, the mutual[5] relations and proportions of number by the arrangement of the seasons and the elements, which renders the earth fertile and productive. He then considered the heavenly bodies, and asserted them to be [6]animated, and endued with 4 perfect wisdom, on account of the regularity and constancy of their motions, so different from those of men. Know, says he, that there are round the [p. 986. A.] whole heaven eight powers, akin to each other (ἀδελ- φὰς ἀλλήλων) one of the sun, one of the moon, &c. Let not any of us suppose, that some of them are

---

[5] Πρὸς ἄλληλα πάντα ἀριθμὸν ἀεὶ λογίζεσθαι—ἀνέμων τε καὶ ὑετῶν γιγνομένων οὐκ ἐξαισίων οὐδὲ ἀμέτρων. [p. 979 A.]

[6] This sentiment is adopted by Philo, Περὶ Κοσμοποιίας, p. 16. ὥσπερ οἱ ἀστέρες· οὗτοι γὰρ ζῷά τε εἶναι λέγονται, καὶ ζῷα νοερά. Origen, who was an admirer of Philo, is thus rendered by his translator Ruffinus in the *Prooemium* to his Treatise Περὶ Ἀρχῶν : "De sole autem et luna et stellis, utrum animantia sint, an exanima, manifeste non traditur.' This, as well as many other opinions of Pythagoras and Plato, appears to have been originally derived from the East. Pococke, in stating Sharestanius's account of the Sabians, who sprung from Chaldea, says, 'it was a tenet of one sect of that religion, that the bodies of the seven planets were the abodes of spiritual beings or intelligences, who possessed them in the same manner, as our bodies are possessed by our souls; and that they are living, rational bodies, animated by intelligences: 'Sacellorum cultores sacella vocant septem planetarum corpora, esse hæc spiritualium seu intelligentiarum habitacula, quæ eodem loco illis sunt, quo animabus nostris corpora. Esseque ea corpora viventia, rationalia, ab intelligentiis animata.' Pocock. *Specimen Hist. Arab.* p. 139. The Indians held this doctrine concerning the fixed stars, and with them agreed the Arabians, *ib.* and p. 163. Vide Maimon. *de Fund. Leg.* p. 33.

gods, and some not—but let us all say, that they are all brothers and in kindred departments—and let us not assign to one the honour of the year, to another the honour of a month, and to others none of that portion of time, in which each performs his course, accomplishing, in conjunction with the others, that visible order which the most divine reason of all established [7]. Inasmuch as that harmony, which is at present to be illustrated, and which produces the year and the seasons (by the contemplation and imitation of which a wise man will attain an harmony of soul, the source of perfect happiness) is not the result of the motions of any of them taken separately, but is the joint effect of all.—In the same manner Plato likewise describes σωφροσύνη in a state, or public virtue, comparing it to ἁρμονία.

De Rep. iv. p. 432. [A.]

Goodness and happiness, both in this world and the next, are to be attained by first admiring this harmony, and then endeavouring to understand and acquire it in ourselves, as far as is possible for human nature. Thus is made out the importance of the knowledge of number, which was taught men by the heaven. Without the

[7] Πάντες δὴ πάντας λέγωμέν τε καὶ φῶμεν ἀδέλφους τ' εἶναι, καὶ ἐν ἀδελφαῖς μοίραις· καὶ τιμὰς [office] ἀποδιδῶμεν, μὴ τῷ μὲν ἐνιαυτόν, τῷ δὲ μῆνα, τοῖς δὲ μήτε τινα μοῖραν τάττωμεν, μήτε τινὰ χρόνον, ἐν ᾧ διεξέρχεται τὸν αὑτοῦ πόλον, ξυναποτελῶν κόσμον, ὃν ἔταξε λόγος ὁ πάντων θειότατος ὁρατόν.

[8] This doctrine is likewise adopted by Philo, Περὶ Κοσμ. p. 17: Τὸ δέ, παντοίων θεαμάτων ἃ καταπληκτικωτάτας μὲν ἔχει τὰς οὐσίας, καταπληκτικωτάτας δὲ τὰς ποιότητας, θαυμασιωτάτας δὲ τὰς κινήσεις καὶ χορείας, ἐν τάξεσιν ἡρμοσμένας καὶ ἀριθμῶν ἀναλογίαις καὶ περιόδων συμφωνίαις. Ἐν οἷς ἅπασι τὴν ἀρχέτυπον

knowledge of number and its proportions there cannot be reason (λόγος), without reason, wisdom, without wisdom an harmony of soul, virtue, and happiness [8].

According to this interpretation of the passage before us, it does not immediately relate to the creation of the world, nor does it at all express the personality of the Logos. Pythagoras first called the world κόσμος, on account of the order and symmetry of its parts. The word is here used in its original signification, and the passage altogether means, that the heavenly bodies, by their regular and well-proportioned motions, conjointly produce that beautiful order, which the divine wisdom marked out. It is to be observed, that the word λόγος, ὃς ἔταξε κόσμον, has not even an article prefixed to it; which, I conceive, it would have had, if it had been intended to express a person.

Nothing is more common in all authors, than to attribute effects to qualities in the abstract without intending to attribute personality to the qualities themselves, or to signify any thing more of them, than that beings, endued with such qualities, have, by the exertion of them, produced such effects [9].

καὶ ἀληθῆ καὶ παραδειγματικὴν μουσικὴν οὐκ ἂν ἁμάρτοι τις εἶναι λέγων· ἀφ' ἧς οἱ μετὰ ταῦτα ἄνθρωποι γραψάμενοι ταῖς ἑαυτῶν ψυχαῖς, ἀναγκαιοτάτην καὶ ὠφελιμωτάτην τέχνην τῷ βίῳ παρέδοσαν.

[9] Thus Cicero, *Le Legibus*, i. 7: Dasne igitur hoc nobis, Pomponi (nam Quinti novi sententiam) Deorum immortalium natura, ratione, potestate, mente, numine, sive quod est aliud verbum, quo planius significem quod volo, naturam omnem regi?—Id, quod tibi concessi, quorsum pertineat, expecto.— Huc pertinet, animal hoc quem vocamus hominem generatum esse a summo Deo—Solum est—particeps rationis—Quid au-

6   EPINOMIS.

p. 988. [D.]
p. 988. [D.]

In the Dialogue before us, Plato, when he speaks of the universe merely as a production, ascribes it to soul (ψυχή), an active and governing principle (ψυχῆς οὔσης αἰτίας τοῦ ὅλου), in opposition to body, which is passive and subject to control (ἀρχόμενον καὶ ἀναίτιον πάσης πάθης). But when he is speaking of the harmony and congruity of the parts of the whole, he assigns it to reason or intelligence, that faculty which is conversant with order and proportion, in opposition to chance or the random tendencies of matter.

The doctrine maintained in this Dialogue, is essentially the same, as that which has been embellished in modern times by the pens of Shaftesbury and Hutcheson, viz. that virtue is founded in a love of order and proportion. It is a doctrine which appears everywhere in the writings of Plato,

---

tem est, non dicam in homine, sed in omni cœlo atque terra, ratione divinius? Quæ cum adolevit, atque perfecta est, nominatur rite sapientia. Again, ii. 13: Cum summos Deos esse concedamus, eorumque mente mundum regi, et eorundem benignitatem hominum consulere generi. And to this same purpose in his Dialogues, *De Nat. Deor.* ii. 38: Quis enim hunc hominem dixerit, qui, cum tam certos cœli motus, tam ratos astrorum ordines, tamque inter se omnia connexa et apta viderit, neget in his ullam inesse rationem, eaque casu fieri dicat, quæ quanto consilio gerantur, nullo consilio adsequi possumus? An cum machinatione quadam moveri aliquid videmus, ut sphæram, ut horas, ut alia permulta; non dubitamus, quin illa opera sint rationis? Cum autem impetum cœli cum admirabili celeritate moveri vertique videamus, constantissime conficientem vicissitudines anniversarias cum summa salute et conservatione rerum omnium; dubitamus, quin ea non solum ratione fiant, sed etiam excellenti divinaque ratione? Xenophon *Memorab.* i. 4. speaks of ἔργα γνώμης and ἔργα προνοίας, which he likewise attributes σοφοῦ τινος δημιούργου καὶ φιλοζώου τεχνήματι.

EPINOMIS. 7

In his Republic[10], he discourses at large upon the importance and connexion of harmony and rhythm in music, arts, and manners. In the same book Plato compares knowledge, passion or anger, and appetite, to the council or senate, the military, and the artizans, &c. in a state. It is the prerogative of knowledge to direct passion, and the duty of passion to aid knowledge in keeping the appetites in subjection; and that harmony, which is the result of their performing each their several functions in due order, constitutes the just and perfect state of the mind of man, and, as it were, the health of the soul. Hence he concludes, that as a city, whose members preserve a regular subordination, will flourish more than one that is torn by contending parties;—and as sound health is better than disease;—so virtue is, on its own account, more desirable than vice.

[10] Τούτων ἕνεκα κυριωτάτη ἐν μουσικῇ τροφή, ὅτι μάλιστα καταδύεται εἰς τὸ ἐντὸς τῆς ψυχῆς ὅ τε ῥυθμὸς καὶ ἁρμονία, καὶ ἐρρωμενέστατα ἅπτεται αὐτῆς, φέροντα τὴν εὐσχημοσύνην· καὶ ποιεῖ εὐσχήμονα, ἐάν τις ὀρθῶς τραφῇ—[καὶ ὅτι αὖ τῶν παραλειπομένων καὶ μὴ καλῶς δημιουργηθέντων ἢ μὴ καλῶς φύντων ὀξύτατ' ἂν αἰσθάνοιτο] ὁ ἐκεῖ τραφεὶς [ὡς ἔδει καὶ ὀρθῶς δὴ δυσχεραίνων] τὰ μὲν καλὰ ἐπαινοῖ, καὶ χαίρων, καὶ καταδεχόμενος εἰς τὴν ψυχὴν τρέφοιτ' ἂν ἀπ' αὐτῶν, καὶ γίγνοιτο καλός τε κἀγαθός: Lib III. p. 401 [D].
Again, Ὁρᾷς οὖν ὅτι ὡς ἁρμονίᾳ τινὶ ἡ σωφροσύνη ὡμοίωται. IV. p. 431 [E].

PARMENIDES.

THE *Parmenides* is perhaps one of the most difficult of the Dialogues of Plato. The expression and the reasoning are so general and abstracted, particularly in the part where ἓν, ἓν πολλά, and ἓν καὶ πολλά are discussed; that it is not easy to determine precisely the meaning of those terms.

Serranus supposes the one infinite Being and second causes to be the subjects of discussion. Other authors, deservedly of great name, have thought that they have discovered the three persons of the ever-blessed Trinity delineated under the articles ἓν, ἓν πολλά, and ἓν καὶ πολλά. Le Clerc, in his *Ars Critica*, P. II. S. I. cxiv, delivers his opinion concerning it in the following terms: *Primus omnium tria principia constituit Parmenides, et post eum Plato; qui an consenserint, non satis liquet, quod Parmenidis non supersit præter obscura fragmenta. Plato autem dixit primum esse τὸ ὄν, αἴτιον ἀπάντων, ens, causam omnium rerum : secundum vero λόγον, Rationem et Rectorem præsentium et futurorum : tertium denique ψυχὴν κόσμου, animam sive spiritum mundi.*

The passages, referred to in support and illustration of this opinion in other parts of Plato's writings, will be considered in their order. I shall at present confine myself to the *Parmenides*, concerning the subjects of which Dialogue Cudworth *Intell. Syst.* pp. 386, 7. had before acceded to the same opinion upon the See p. 546, &c. authority of Plotinus, as appears from the following extract: " Wherefore Parmenides his whole philosophy (saith Plotinus) was better digested, and more exactly and distinctly set down in Plato's *Parmenides*, where he acknowledgeth three Unities subordinate, or a Trinity of divine hypostases. Which observation of Plotinus is, by the way, the best key, that we know of, for that obscure book of Plato's *Parmenides*" The last part of the quotation seems to me to imply that he accepted this key, not because he was perfectly satisfied with it, but because he knew of no other so good for unlocking the intricacies of that obscure book. He in fact appears to have considered it as the most plausible hypothesis that had fallen in his way. If, therefore, we can obtain a key from the book itself, which will unlock its intricacies in a manner consistent with the subject of the discourse, with the train of reasoning adopted in it, with the philosophic principles of the characters introduced, and with the manner of their applying those principles; I am persuaded that every judicious reader will acknowledge such a key to be infinitely more valuable, than any arbitrary hypothesis of Plotinus, however specious it may have appeared, before this key was presented to him.

Before I enter upon the investigation, it will be proper to observe, that Parmenides is the chief speaker of the Dialogue; and that the principles, advanced in it, are the principles of that philosopher, from whom Plato differed in opinion on some particular points, as we are told by Aristotle.

Let it be no objection to this observation, that the discourse was held in the presence of Socrates, that he bore a part in the beginning of it, and that he was in a great degree the occasion of the whole. Socrates was the master of Plato; and the sentiments and reasonings which are assigned to him, may in general be safely considered as the sentiments and reasonings of Plato himself. It was likewise the usual custom, and indeed the chief employment of Socrates, to correct what he saw amiss in the practice and opinions of those with whom he conversed; and, above all, to detect the fallacious principles, and refute the false reasonings of the philosophers and sophists of his time. His express approbation, therefore, and his tacit aquiescence, had commonly the same tendency, though perhaps not so often the same force.

But upon the present occasion, Socrates is represented in a situation, in which he does not often appear in the works of Plato. He is introduced in this Dialogue at a time of life when he was not a teacher, but a learner; when it was customary with him, as he tells us in his *Phædo*, to attend the different philosophers of distinguished note; in order that he might be able, by impartial observation, to discover whose doctrine was most consistent with the reality of things, and of course, under whose guidance he should put himself in his future inquiries. It was not till he despaired of receiving any effectual assistance from others, that he struck out a method of philosophizing peculiarly his own. In this Dialogue, therefore, contrary to what is the case in most others, we must not consider the acquiescence and approbation of Socrates as the same.

Yet even here Plato appears to treat his master with exquisite delicacy. He makes him indeed propose his objections to the principles of Zeno, and defend the consequences deduced from those objections with an ingenuousness suitable to his age; and he at length makes him, with the same ingenuousness, acknowledge himself confounded by his veteran antagonist, who was by long practice versed in all the subtleties of disputation. But when Parmenides is prevailed upon to explain his own principles, the office of replying, and of course either of opposing or of expressing an acquiescence, is transferred to Aristotle; and Socrates takes no part in the remainder of the Dialogue.

I have thought it necessary to make these observations, lest any one should think, that it is a serious objection to the interpretation here produced, if the principles attributed to Parmenides should seem not always exactly to agree with the principles maintained by Plato under the character of Socrates, in other parts of his writings. I will now proceed to examine the Dialogue itself.

Among the persons of the Dialogue was Parmenides, an old philosopher, who had maintained ἓν εἶναι τὸ πᾶν, [1]'that the universe is one thing'; by which, I conceive, he meant one system; and that all the things which subsist have a mutual connexion with each other, and subsist in it as parts of one whole. Zeno was a friend of Parmenides, and some years younger than himself. He had maintained, οὐ πολλὰ εἶναι, 'that it is not many', does not consist of separate unconnected parts. Socrates, then a youth, was desirous of knowing the meaning and foundation of those doctrines, which Zeno affirmed not to be precisely the same, though his reasoning operated as a defence of the doctrine of his friend.

The first point which demands our attention, is to discover what is the real subject of the Dialogue. The nature of the objection urged by Socrates, the reply to it by Parmenides, and the defence of it afterwards by Socrates, deserve our serious consideration; as they may fairly be supposed to be founded upon the subject of debate.— As so many parts enter into the composition of the universe, it is obvious, that, if it can be denominated one thing, it must be so, because it is capable of being comprehended under one εἶδος or general abstract form. Now the difficulty that occurred to Socrates in the doctrine of Zeno, which

---

[1] It is probable, that his theological opinion did not essentially differ from that of Thales: ΘΑΛΗΣ νοῦν τοῦ κόσμου τὸν θεόν· τὸ δὲ πᾶν ἔμψυχον ἅμα καὶ δαιμόνων πλῆρες. Stobæi *Eclogæ Physicæ*, I. [2. § 29]. This was also the great outline of the theology of the Stoics.

[2] Οὐ νομίζεις εἶναι αὐτὸ καθ᾽ αὑτὸ εἶδός τι ὁμοιότητος, καὶ τῷ τοιούτῳ αὖ ἄλλο τι ἐναντίον, ὃ ἔστι ἀνόμοιον; τούτοιν δὲ, δυοῖν

denies a plurality, was this, that there are many distinct [2] εἴδη, general abstract forms, each subsisting separately and independently. What does Parmenides reply to this? Does he say, You mistake the nature of the thing or being, the unity of which I maintain? No. He undertakes to shew the contradictions, which, according to his reasoning, would arise from supposing, that the several εἴδη, 'species' or general abstract forms, subsist unconnectedly, and in a manner that is inconsistent with the unity of τὸ πᾶν, 'the universe'[3].

I am well persuaded that the language and mode of reasoning adopted in this Dialogue, will appear very harsh and forced to modern apprehensions, which are more conversant and better pleased with the dictates of sound sense confined within its proper limits, than with the logical subtilties of ancient metaphysics. But if we would arrive at the genuine sense of an author, we must be contented to accompany him upon his own terms, and to reason with him upon his own principles.

The specimen, which I have produced, will perhaps be sufficient to convince most people that I have rightly stated *the subject* of the debate. If

ὄντοιν, καὶ ἐμὲ καὶ σὲ καὶ τὰ ἄλλα, ἃ δὴ πολλὰ καλοῦμεν, μεταλαμβάνειν; καὶ τὰ μὲν, τῆς ὁμοιότητος μεταλαμβάνοντα, ὅμοια γίγνεσθαι, ταύτῃ τε καὶ κατὰ τοσοῦτον, ὅσον ἂν μεταλαμβάνῃ; τὰ δὲ τῆς ἀνομοιότητος ἀνόμοια; [p. 128 E.]

[3] Ὁρᾶς οὖν, φάναι, ὦ Σώκρατες, ὅση ᾖ ἀπορία, ἐάν τις ὡς εἴδη ὄντα αὐτὰ καθ' ἑαυτὰ διορίζηται. [p. 133 A.]

any be yet doubtful concerning it, I would recommend it to them, to peruse with attention the whole of the conversation, if I may so call it, between Parmenides and Socrates, as it is set down at large in the original. Will they then be able to believe, that Socrates found a difficulty in acknowledging a perfect Unity, or in denying a plurality in the Deity, as distinct from the Universe; because he supposed different abstract forms of equality and inequality, of greatness, justice, beauty, and the like, to subsist by themselves separately and independently of each other, and severally to belong, either connectedly or disjunctively, to the several individual external Actions or Beings? Will they be able, in the next place, to conceive, that Parmenides, instead of urging the want of connexion between the doctrine and the objection, should undertake to point out the inconsistencies that would arise from admitting the truth of the opinion upon which the objection is built; and that the whole of the following conversation should be employed, on one part, in endeavouring to explain away those inconsistencies; and on the other part, to shew the insufficiency of the explanations, and the still greater difficulties, that would result from them? If, besides conceiving and believing all this, they can think it possible, that the discourse should be carried on through so many debates, objections, replies, and rejoinders, without either party mentioning, or in the most distant manner alluding to the real and original subject of doubt and dispute; I confess,

PARMENIDES. 15

I know of no argument or mode of reasoning that is capable of reaching them. When Socrates seemed disposed to acknowledge that he was puzzled with the difficulty of the question, Parmenides told him that he had plunged into the depths of philosophy in the morning of life, before he was sufficiently exercised. He praised indeed his ingenuity, but recommended it to him to exercise himself first in the discussion of more simple topics; by which means he would afterwards be able with less difficulty to investigate more intricate and complicated subjects. The kind of exercise which Parmenides recommended, as suited to the present state of Socrates, was hypothetical reasoning both positively and negatively upon the same subject. For instance, ⁴If a thing be *so*, what will be the consequence? Again, If a thing be *not so*, what will be the consequence? After some entreaty, Parmenides is prevailed upon to give Socrates a specimen of what he meant. He says, ⁵he will begin from himself and an hypothesis of the truth of his own tenet, which was the unity of the Universe, ἓν εἶναι τὸ πᾶν. Concerning which he will enquire, first, If it be true: secondly, If it be not true, what will be the consequence.

---

⁴ Χρὴ δὲ καὶ τόδε ἔτι πρὸς τούτῳ ποιεῖν, μὴ μόνον, εἰ ἔστιν ἕκαστον ὑποτιθέμενον, σκοπεῖν τὰ συμβαίνοντα ἐκ τῆς ὑποθέσεως, ἀλλὰ καὶ εἰ μή ἐστι τὸ αὐτὸ τοῦτο ὑποτίθεσθαι, εἰ βούλει μᾶλλον γυμνασθῆναι. [p. 135 E.]

⁵ [Βούλεσθε] ἀπ' ἐμοῦ ἄρχωμαι καὶ τῆς ἐμαυτοῦ ὑποθέσεως, περὶ τοῦ ἑνὸς αὐτοῦ ὑποθέμενος, εἴ τε ἕν ἐστιν, εἴ τε μὴ ἕν, τί χρὴ ξυμβαίνειν. [p. 137 B.]

From the hypothesis of his tenet with respect to unity being true, he shews, first, that unity itself in its most simple state, as it is predicated of the Universe, indicates nothing beyond itself but mere unity. It contains no other quality whatever. It implies neither beginning, nor end, nor shape, nor identity, nor diversity, nor time, nor place, nor existence, nor non-existence, nor any other property. Secondly, if in the hypothesis of unity be included existence, which must be the case when you come to consider the several parts that are comprehended under this most simple unity, and as it were tied together by it, an infinite multitude will immediately branch out from it. For the unity according to the hypothesis thus stated will imply existence, and existence unity; so that they necessarily become

[6] Τό τε γὰρ ἓν τὸ ὂν ἀεὶ ἴσχει, καὶ τὸ ὂν τὸ ἕν, ὥστε ἀνάγκη, δύ' ἀεὶ γιγνόμενον, μηδέποτε ἓν εἶναι—οὐκοῦν ἄπειρον ἂν τὸ πλῆθος οὕτω τὸ ἓν ὂν εἴη, [p. 143 A.] This will appear very peculiar reasoning to those, who have not some acquaintance with the language of ancient metaphysics. But Aristotle tells us, that this verb, ἐστί, *is*, by its efficacy to destroy the unity of unit in being predicated of it, gave such disturbance to the philosophers, who maintained an unity of principle, that some of them, as Lycophron, struck it out. Others changed the form of the expression; as, for instance, they would not say, The man *is* walking, but, The man walks; lest, by applying the word *is*, they should make one thing to be many. As if, says Aristotle, unity and existence were expressed only in one manner: Ἐθορυβοῦντο δὲ καὶ οἱ ὕστεροι, καθάπερ οἱ ἀρχαῖοι, μή ποτε συμβαίνῃ αὐτοῖς ἅμα τὸ αὐτὸ ἓν εἶναι καὶ πολλά. Διὸ οἱ μὲν τὸ ἔστιν ἀφεῖλον, ὥσπερ Λυκόφρων· οἱ δὲ τὴν λέξιν μετερρύθμιζον, ὅτι ὁ ἄνθρωπος οὐ λευκός ἐστιν ἀλλὰ λελεύκωται, οὐδὲ βαδίζων ἐστὶν, ἀλλὰ βαδίζει· ἵνα μὴ, τὸ ἔστι προσάπτοντες, πολλὰ εἶναι ποιῶσι τὸ ἕν, ὡς μοναχῶς λεγομένου τοῦ ἑνὸς ἢ τοῦ ὄντος.—*Natur. Auscult.* Lib. I. [Ch. 2. *ed. Bekk.*] Plato in *Thecetetus* gives a similar account of the

two, and consequently can be no longer one[6]. Now 19 says he, unity, when by the hypothesis it partakes of existence, becomes many; though, when it is contemplated alone by the understanding in its simple state, it appears only an unit[7]. This reasoning of our author is thus ridiculed by Theopompus, ἓν γάρ ἐστι οὐδὲ ἕν· τὰ δὲ δύο μόλις ἕν ἐστιν, ὥς φησι Πλάτων. [Diog. Laert. [Vitæ. Philos. Lib.III. Segm. 26.] Moreover, not only ἕν, when it partakes of οὐσία, 'existence', will become many in number, that is, branch out into an infinite multitude of units or species; but also each of those will be rendered limited in its nature, (πεπερασμένον ἂν εἴη) distinguished by a particular form. The specific forms, thus infinite in multitude, though they branch out from ἕν, 'unit'[8], and centre in it, will be

doctrine of some philosophers concerning the material elements: Ἐγὼ γὰρ αὖ ἐδόκουν ἀκούειν τινῶν, ὅτι τὰ μὲν πρῶτα οἱαπερεὶ στοιχεῖα, ἐξ ὧν ἡμεῖς τε συγκείμεθα καὶ τἆλλα, λόγον οὐκ ἔχοι· αὐτὸ γὰρ καθ' αὑτὸ ἕκαστον ὀνομάσαι μόνον εἴη, προσειπεῖν δὲ οὐδὲν ἄλλο δυνατόν, οὔθ' ὡς ἔστιν, οὔθ' ὡς οὐκ ἔστιν· ἤδη γὰρ ἂν οὐσίαν, ἢ μὴ οὐσίαν αὐτῷ προστίθεσθαι. δεῖν δὲ οὐδὲν προσφέρειν, εἴπερ αὐτὸ ἐκεῖνο μόνον τις ἐρεῖ, p. 201, 2.

[7] Αὐτὸ τὸ ἕν, ὃ δή φαμεν οὐσίας μετέχειν, ἐὰν αὐτὸ τῇ διανοίᾳ μόνον καθ' αὑτὸ λάβωμεν, ἄνευ τούτου, οὗ φαμὲν μετέχειν, ἆρά γε ἓν μόνον φανήσεται ἢ καὶ πολλὰ τὸ αὐτὸ τοῦτο; ἕν, οἶμαι ἔγωγε, [p. 143 A.]

[8] Plato in the *Philebus* explains at large the process of reducing many distinct things to one. Things, which in their own nature admit of more or less, such as hot, cold, swift, slow, &c., are not only many and various, but also opposite to each other. Yet being collected and classed under the genus of unlimited, they become one. Or, as he expressed it again, The unlimited presented many genera; but being impressed with the genus of more and its opposite, it appeared one: Πολλά γε καὶ τὸ ἄπειρον παρέσχετο γένη· ὅμως δ' ἐπισφραγισθέντα τῷ τοῦ

not only different, but often directly opposite to each other, and thus express all the qualities that can come under observation; limited in their nature, as being severally one, and confined to a particular and appropriated form; and unlimited in number, as there is many a one: καὶ πεπερασμένον καὶ ἄπειρον πλήθει.

Again, after ἓν πολλά, many species, each of which is properly an unit, partaking of existence and limited in its form, there arise from the hypothesis the several particulars in nature one and many (ἓν καὶ πολλά) connected with time, and partly partaking of existence and partly not[9]. These individuals, subject to generation and destruction, are unlimited both in number and in nature[10]. The specific form gives them a limitation in their relation to other species; while their own nature produces an unlimited variety in the particulars of the same species.

This will receive illustration from the *Philebus*, in which Dialogue Plato makes Socrates divide the

μᾶλλον καὶ ἐναντίου γένει ἐν ἐφάνη, p. 26 [D]. How much more easy is it, says he, to reduce under one head those things, which by their nature are limited, and are not severally many! Καὶ μὴν τό γε πέρας οὔτε πολλὰ εἶχεν, οὔτ' ἐδυσκολαίνομεν ὡς οὐκ ἦν ἐν φύσει.—*Ib.*

[9] Τὸ ἓν εἰ ἔστιν, οἷον διεληλύθαμεν, ἆρ' οὐκ ἀνάγκη αὐτό, ἕν τε ὂν καὶ πολλὰ, καὶ μήτε ἓν μήτε πολλὰ, καὶ μέτεχον χρόνου, ὅτι μὲν ἔστιν ἕν, οὐσίας μετέχειν ποτέ; ὅτι δὲ οὐκ ἔστι, μὴ μετέχειν αὖ ποτε οὐσίας, [p. 155 E.] They are called ἓν καὶ πολλά, as consisting of idea or form, which is one, and matter, which is denominated many.

[10] Οὐκοῦν οὕτως ἀεὶ σκοποῦντι αὐτὴν καθ' αὑτὴν τὴν ἑτέραν φύσιν τοῦ εἴδους, ὅσον ἂν αὐτῆς ἀεὶ ὁρῶμεν, ἄπειρον ἔσται πλήθει ;—Τοῖς ἄλλοις δὴ τοῦ ἑνὸς συμβαίνει, ἐκ μὲν τοῦ ἑνὸς καὶ ἐξ ἑαυτῶν κοινω-

principles of things into two kinds. First, matter and its qualities, which admitting in its own nature degrees of more and less, and having nothing in its nature to confine those qualities, he calls ἄπειρον, 'unlimited'. Secondly, specific form, which containing in its own nature a principle of limitation, he calls πέρας, and ἔχον πέρας[11]. The first he likewise calls πολλά, as being many in its nature[12]. But the latter is opposed to it as being characteristically different; since it does not admit of that denomination in its nature[13]. Though he had[14] before said that each kind is divided into many in number. Out of these two conjoined arises a third class, which comprises all particular things[15].

22 Of this union he produces several instances: among others, in disorders a proper limitation, applied to the constituent parts of the body, produces health[16]. Again, limitation being applied to sharp, flat, swift, and slow sounds, which are in their own nature unlimited, constitutes music.

νησάντων, ὡς ἔοικεν, ἕτερόν τι γίγνεσθαι ἐν αὐτοῖς, ὃ δὴ πέρας πάρεσχε πρὸς ἄλληλα· ἡ δὲ αὐτῶν φύσις καθ' ἑαυτὰ, ἀπειρίαν. [p. 158 c.]
[11] Τὸν Θεὸν ἐλέγομέν που τὸ μὲν ἄπειρον δεῖξαι τῶν ὄντων, τὸ δὲ πέρας. [p. 23 c.]
[12] Ὅτι δὲ τρόπον τινὰ τὸ ἄπειρον πολλά ἐστι πειράσομαι φράζειν. [p. 24 A.]
[13] Καὶ μὴν τόγε πέρας οὔτε πολλὰ εἶχεν. [p. 26 D.]
[14] Τὰ δύο τούτων πειρώμεθα πολλὰ ἑκάτερον ἐσχισμένον καὶ διεσπασμένον ἰδόντες, εἰς ἓν πάλιν ἑκάτερον συναγαγόντες. p. 23 [E].
[15] Τὸ δὲ τρίτον ἐξ ἀμφοῖν τούτοιν ἕν τι ξυμμισγόμενον.
[16] Ἆρ' οὐκ ἐν μὲν νόσοις ἡ τούτων ὀρθὴ κοινωνία τὴν ὑγιείας φύσιν ἐγέννησε; p. 25 [E].

Plato, in the fifth Book of his *Republic*, has put into the mouth of Socrates a doctrine of εἴδη, 'species', similar to what is here laid down. 'Since', says he, 'handsome and ugly are opposite to each other, they are collectively two, but separately one. The same may be said of just and unjust, of good and evil, and all species. They are each separately one, though by a participation of actions and bodies, and of each other, they appear severally to be many'[17]. 'These', he says, 'consisting partly of 23 existence and partly of non-existence, are the objects of opinion (δόξα), that holds a middle place between knowledge, which embraces essential forms, and ignorance, to which absolute non-entities are assigned'.

When Parmenides had shewn that the present state of things would result from the positive hypothesis of the unity of the universe; he proceeded to argue upon the negative hypothesis, which was found to lead to very different conclusions.

The reasoning of Parmenides is founded upon the abstract nature of an unit, and is intended to shew, that the present state of things results from the unity of the universe. Hence if this reasoning

[17] Ἐπειδή ἐστιν ἐναντίον καλὸν αἰσχρῷ, δύο αὐτὼ εἶναι. πῶς δ' οὔ; οὐκοῦν, ἐπειδὴ δύο, καὶ ἓν ἑκάτερον. Καὶ τοῦτο. Καὶ περὶ δικαίου καὶ ἀδίκου, καὶ ἀγαθοῦ καὶ κακοῦ, καὶ πάντων τῶν εἰδῶν πέρι ὁ αὐτὸς λόγος· αὐτὸ μὲν, ἓν ἕκαστον εἶναι, τῇ δὲ τῶν πραξέων καὶ σωμάτων καὶ ἀλλήλων κοινωνίᾳ πανταχοῦ φανταζόμενα, πολλὰ φαίνεσθαι ἕκαστον, p. 467 [A]. Again in the tenth book: Εἶδος γάρ πού τι ἓν ἕκαστον εἰώθαμεν τίθεσθαι περὶ ἕκαστα τὰ πολλὰ, οἷς ταὐτὸν ὄνομα ἐπιφέρομεν. ἢ οὐ μανθάνεις; Μανθάνω. Θῶμεν δὴ καὶ νῦν ὅ,τι βούλει τῶν πολλῶν. οἷον, εἰ θέλεις, πολλαί πού εἰσι κλῖναι καὶ τράπεζαι. Πῶς δ' οὔ; Ἀλλὰ ἰδέαι γέ που περὶ

were allowed, the necessity of a Creator would be superseded, and the universe, considered as a whole, would have the principle of existence in itself, be independent and eternal.

Aristotle, in his Φυσική ακρόασις, examines the opinions of the different philosophers concerning the principles of things. In the second chapter of the first book he accuses Melissus and Parmenides of assuming false principles, and of reasoning unsyllogistically from them. He says, that the assumption of their first principle was inconsistent with an investigation of nature; that a true natural philosopher could no more dispute with them, than a geometrician could dispute with one who denied the first principles of geometry. The force of the objection consisted in this, that they deduced a system of physics from a metaphysical principle. In the following chapter he urges the absurdity of treating unit as a principle of production, which is considering that as a substance, which in itself expresses only quantity or number. In the first chapter of the thirteenth book of his *Metaphysics*, Aristotle himself acknowledges unity and existence to be true metaphysical principles

ταῦτα τὰ σκεύη δύο· μία μὲν κλίνης, μία δὲ τραπέζης, p. 596 [B].
In the latter of which passages in particular it is to be observed, that several εἴδη or ἰδέαι are said to be πολλὰ, many in number, and the particulars classed under each ἰδέα are τὰ πολλὰ, 'the many,' and that each separate εἶδος or ἰδέα is ἐν ἕκαστον περὶ ἕκαστα τὰ πολλά. Thus Aristotle, stating the difference of the language that was held by Plato, and some other philosophers, concerning the principles of things, says, Ὁ μὲν (Πλάτων) ταῦτα ποιεῖ ὕλην, τὸ δὲ ἓν τὸ εἶδος· οἱ δὲ τὸ μὲν ἓν τὸ ὑποκείμενον ὕλην, τὰ δὲ ἐναντία διαφορὰς καὶ εἴδη.—*Nat. Ausc.* I. 5. [Ch. 4. ed. *Bekker*.]

and to comprehend all subsisting beings: πᾶς γὰρ λόγος καὶ πᾶσα ἐπιστήμη τῶν καθόλου καὶ οὐ τῶν ἐσχάτων, ὥστ᾽ εἴη ἂν οὕτω τῶν πρώτων γένων· ταῦτα δὲ γίγνοιτ᾽ ἄν τό τε ὂν καὶ τὸ ἕν· ταῦτα γὰρ μάλιστ᾽ ἂν ὑποληφθείη περιέχειν τὰ ὄντα πάντα.

PLATO'S
DOCTRINE OF IDEAS.

IT may not be improper in this place to say something of Plato's general doctrine of *Ideas*. He divided all objects into two grand classes, denominated, from the different methods by which we become acquainted with them, rather than from their own nature, *Intelligibles* and *Sensibles*: (νοητὰ καὶ αἰσθητά.) The first are the objects of the understanding, and the other of the senses[1]. The intelligibles, which were single in their several kinds (ἓν ἕκαστον), were considered as the only real existences and the objects of knowledge. The sensibles, which were the many (τὰ πολλὰ), being of a very different description, were the foundations of opinion only.

Under the class of sensibles he comprehended not only every particular external object, of what kind soever, but also every particular act or concrete quality belonging to it. There were many beautiful, many good, and many just things (πολλὰ καλά, πολλὰ ἀγαθά, καὶ πολλὰ δίκαια), which were all classed under sensibles (αἰσθητά); since the notice of all particulars is conveyed by the senses. But the intelligibles (τὰ νοητὰ) were those things which are to be comprehended only by the under-

[1] Τὰ μὲν δὴ ὁρᾶσθαί φαμεν, νοεῖσθαι δ' οὔ· τὰς δ' αὖ ἰδέας νοεῖσθαι μέν, ὁρᾶσθαι δ' οὔ.—*De Rep.* VI. p. 507 [B].

standing with reason[2]. In this class were included not only spiritual substances, but also all general abstract qualities (τ. ε. τὸ ἀγαθὸν καὶ τὸ δίκαιον.) So that, in fact, ἓν ἕκαστον νοητὸν was the general or abstract idea, and τὰ πολλὰ αἰσθητὰ the several particulars arranged under it. Aristotle, who viewed nature with a more curious eye, and who was not so much under the influence of a lively and refined imagination, formed a very different judgment upon the subject. He maintained that bodily or material objects were most properly entities[3]. He divided entities (οὐσίαι) into *primary* and *secondary*. By primary entities he meant particulars, as a particular man or a particular horse. By secondary entities he meant the species and genus, under which the particulars are classed. Thus the primary entity is a particular man: and the secondary entities are the species man and the genus animal[4]. His doctrine, therefore, is in this respect directly opposite to that of his master. For he maintains

---

[2] Νοήσει μετὰ λόγου περιληπτόν.—*Timæus*, p. 28 [A].

[3] Οὐσίαι δὲ μάλιστ' εἶναι δοκοῦσι τὰ σώματα.—*De Anima*, II. 1. And again: Λέγω δ' οὐσίας μὲν τά τε ἁπλᾶ σώματα, οἷον πῦρ καὶ γῆν, καὶ ὅσα σύστοιχα τούτοις, καὶ ὅσα ἐκ τούτων.—*De Cœlo*, III. 1.

[4] Δεύτεραι δὲ οὐσίαι λέγονται ἐν οἷς εἴδεσιν αἱ πρώτως οὐσίαι λεγόμεναι ὑπάρχουσι· ταῦτά τε καὶ τὰ τῶν εἰδῶν τούτων γένη· οἷον, ὁ τὶς ἄνθρωπος ἐν εἴδει μὲν ὑπάρχει τῷ ἀνθρώπῳ· γένος δὲ τοῦ εἴδους ἐστὶ τὸ ζῶον· δεύτεραι οὖν αὗται λέγονται οὐσίαι, οἷον ὅ τε ἄνθρωπος καὶ τὸ ζῶον.—*Categor*. 5.

[5] Αἱ πρῶται οὐσίαι, διὰ τὸ τοῖς ἄλλοις ἅπασιν ὑποκεῖσθαι—κυριώτατα οὐσίαι λέγονται—Μὴ οὐσῶν οὖν τῶν πρώτων οὐσιῶν, ἀδύνατον τῶν ἄλλων τι εἶναι.—*Ibid*.

[6] Πᾶσα δὲ οὐσία δοκεῖ τόδε τι σημαίνειν· ἐπὶ μὲν οὖν τῶν

PLATO'S *Doctrine of Ideas.*

that particulars are the only proper entities: that the species and genus exist only in a secondary sense; and that they could not exist at all, were it not for the particulars or primary entities[5]. Now, says he, an entity seems to point out some actual and particular thing, which a primary entity truly and indisputably does. Indeed by the construction of the sentence a secondary entity *appears* to do so, but does not in reality. It expresses only the quality[6].

The reason why many philosophers held general ideas to be the real entities, was, as Aristotle very justly observed[7], that they regarded particular objects as transitory and fleeting. On this account Plato characterizes his entities as always the same, and permanent in their nature and relations to each other (ἀεὶ κατὰ τὰ αὐτὰ καὶ ὡσαύτως ἔχοντα). In the *Philebus* he divides knowledge into two kinds: First, experimental knowledge, which he places in a secondary class, as being conversant about fluctuating and perishable things.

πρώτων οὐσίων ἀναμφισβήτητον καὶ ἀληθές ἐστιν ὅτι τόδε τι σημαίνει—ἄτομον γὰρ καὶ ἐν ἀριθμῷ τὸ δηλούμενόν ἐστιν. ἐπὶ δὲ τῶν δευτέρων οὐσιῶν φαίνεται μὲν ὁμοίως τῷ σχήματι τῆς προσηγορίας τόδε τι σημαίνειν, ὅταν εἴπῃ ἄνθρωπον ἢ ζῷον· οὐ μὴν ἀληθές γε· ἀλλὰ μᾶλλον ποιόν τι σημαίνει· οὐ γὰρ [ἐν inserit Bekker] ἐστὶ τὸ ὑποκείμενον, ὥσπερ ἡ πρώτη οὐσία, ἀλλὰ κατὰ πολλῶν ὁ ἄνθρωπος λέγεται καὶ τὸ ζῷον.—*Ibid.*

[7] Τὰ μὲν οὖν ἐν τοῖς αἰσθητοῖς καθέκαστα ῥεῖν ἐνόμιζον καὶ μένειν οὐδὲν αὐτῶν.—*Metaph.* xi. 12. Συνέβη δ' ἡ περὶ τῶν εἰδῶν δόξα τοῖς εἰποῦσι, διὰ τὸ πεισθῆναι περὶ τῆς ἀληθείας τοῖς Ἡρακλειτείοις λόγοις, ὡς πάντων τῶν αἰσθητῶν ἀεὶ ῥεόντων. ὥστ', εἴπερ ἐπιστήμη τινὸς ἔσται καὶ φρόνησις, ἑτέρας δεῖν τινας φύσεις εἶναι παρὰ τὰς αἰσθητὰς μενούσας; οὐ γὰρ εἶναι τῶν ῥεόντων ἐπιστήμην.—*Ib.* cap. 4.

Secondly, abstract knowledge, which is entitled to the first class, as it respects things unchangeable and permanent[8].

Περὶ τῶν
Χερουβίμ,
p. 116, § 15.

Philo Judæus, no inconsiderable Platonist, founds a curious interpretation of Scripture upon this doctrine of Plato. He says that the sacred writings on this account style God the husband, not of a virgin; for that is changeable and mortal —but of virginity, which is of a permanent nature[9].

[8] Ἐπιστήμη δὴ ἐπιστήμης διάφορος, ἡ μὲν ἐπὶ τὰ γιγνόμενα καὶ ἀπολλύμενα ἀποβλέπουσα, ἡ δὲ ἐπὶ τὰ μήτε γιγνόμενα μήτε ἀπολλύμενα, κατὰ ταὐτὰ δὲ καὶ ὡσαύτως ὄντα ἀεί. ταύτην εἰς τὸ ἀληθὲς ἐπισκοπούμενοι ἡγησάμεθα ἐκείνης ἀληθεστέραν εἶναι, p. 61 [D]. This is similar to what he had said a little before; Τὴν περὶ τὸ ὂν καὶ τὸ ὄντως καὶ τὸ κατὰ ταὐτὸν ἀεὶ πεφυκός, πάντως ἔγωγε οἶμαι ἡγεῖσθαι ξύμπαντας ὅσοις νοῦ καὶ σμικρὸν προσήρτηται, μακρῷ ἀληθεστάτην εἶναι γνῶσιν, p. 58 [A].

[9] Διόπερ ὁ χρησμὸς [Jerem. iii. 4.] πεφύλακται θεὸν ἄνδρα εἰπών, οὐ παρθένου—τρεπτὴ γὰρ ἥδε καὶ θνητή—ἀλλὰ παρθενίας, τῆς ἀεὶ κατὰ τὰ αὐτὰ καὶ ὡσαύτως ἐχούσης ἰδέας.

CONCERNING ΤΟ ΑΓΑΘΟΝ.

WE will now examine what Plato has discoursed in his Treatise *De Republica*, περὶ τῆς τοῦ ἀγαθοῦ ἰδέας, which he calls μέγιστον μάθημα. As Plotinus, Cudworth, and many others, suppose τὸ ἀγαθόν to mean the Supreme Being[1], it will be proper to consider it with some attention. [*Intellectual System*, pp. 259, 407 foll.]

We know that all the sects of heathen philosophers did, with the greatest reason, look upon the question concerning the Greatest Good[2] as one of the most important that could engage their attention. Cicero, in his Treatise concerning *Laws*, which he wrote in imitation of Plato, says, that the question is immediately connected with that subject; as it is the business of him who draws the plan of a State always to have an eye to the greatest good of the subjects, which he can never do, unless he knows wherein that good consists. [*De Legg.* Lib. i. cap. 3.]

But let us observe in what manner Plato makes

---

[1] Brucker seems to think that Plato here describes the second hypostasis in the divine nature. *Historia Critica Philosophiæ*, Pars II. Lib. II. 6. § 1.

[2] Quid est enim in vita tanto opere quærendum, quam cum omnia in philosophia, tum id, quod his Libris quæritur, quid sit finis, quid extremum, quid ultimum, quo sint omnia bene vivendi recteque faciendi consilia referenda? quid sequatur natura ut summum ex rebus expetendis, quid fugiat ut extremum malorum? Qua de re cum sit inter doctissimos summa dissensio, etc.—*De Finibus*, I. 4.

Socrates enter upon this discourse περὶ τῆς τοῦ ἀγαθοῦ ἰδέας, or, as he elsewhere calls it, to discover what is the most excellent of human possessions or acquirements: πρὸς τὸ διελέσθαι τί τῶν ἀνθρωπίνων κτημάτων ἄριστον.

He states it as the most difficult and at the same time the most important attainment; without which indeed every other possession and attainment would be of no value[3]. Having warned his hearers of the difficulty and importance of the question, he proceeds to state the opinions of others concerning it. The multitude think it to be pleasure; but those who are more refined, esteem it to be knowledge or wisdom[4]. The subject of enquiry, therefore, was plainly that which Cicero calls *controversam rem et plenam dissensionis inter doctissimos*[5], and which he describes to be that to which all things are referred, and for the sake of obtaining which all things are to be done[6]. Hence, it appears that it must have been what the nature of the enquiry implies, and what all philosophers, how much soever they differed in other respects, esteemed it, either the possession of some external object capable of being enjoyed, or some personal qualifications, either corporeal or mental, capable of the most

---

[3] *Ἦ οἴει τι πλέον εἶναι πᾶσαν κτῆσιν ἐκτῆσθαι, μὴ μέντοι ἀγαθήν; ἢ πάντα τἆλλα φρονεῖν [ἄνευ τοῦ ἀγαθοῦ] καλὸν δὲ καὶ ἀγαθὸν μηδὲν φρονεῖν;* VI. p. 505 [B].

[4] Τοῖς μὲν πολλοῖς ἡδονὴ δοκεῖ εἶναι τὸ ἀγαθόν, τοῖς δὲ κομψοτέροις φρόνησις. [*Ibid.*]

[5] These are terms very similar to those which Socrates uses in speaking of it: οὐκοῦν ὅτι μὲν μεγάλαι καὶ πολλαὶ ἀμφισβητήσεις περὶ αὐτοῦ φανερόν. [*Ibid.* D.]

perfect enjoyment, or a mixture of those several ingredients[7].

Socrates was asked again, whether he thought the greatest good to be knowledge, or pleasure, or something else different from those[8]. He told them that he could not display to them τὸ ἀγαθόν itself; but he would set before them its offspring most like itself, which he afterwards explained to be knowledge in the mind and truth in things. By which I conceive him to mean, that τὸ ἀγαθόν, the most general idea of good, must be an abstract of the universal good, an object infinitely beyond the capacity of the human intellect, at least in the present state of man; but that some resemblance of it may be attained by knowledge exercised upon the truth of things. These, he says, are not τὸ [p. 509.] ἀγαθόν, but ἀγαθοειδῆ. They spring from the universal good. In the *Second Alcibiades*, Socrates is [p. 145 E.] made to ask what kind of state that would be which should be composed of men skilled in all other arts and sciences ἄνευ τῆς τοῦ βελτίστου ἐπιστήμης. Alcibiades is soon prevailed upon to acknowledge that it would be a state of the greatest confusion and anarchy: Ἆρ' οὐκ ἂν ὀρθῶς λέγοιμεν, φάντες [p. 146 D.] πολλῆς ταραχῆς τε καὶ ἀνομίας μεστὴν εἶναι τὴν τοιαύτην πολιτείαν.

[6] Finem bonorum, quo referuntur omnia, et cujus apiscendi causa sunt facienda omnia.—*De Legg.* I. 20. Or, in the language of Plato, ὃ δὴ διώκει μὲν ἅπασα ψυχὴ, καὶ τούτου ἕνεκα πάντα πράττει.

[7] Τἀγαθὸν δὲ οἰκεῖόν τι καὶ δυσαφαίρετον.—Arist. *Ethic. Nicom.* I. 3.

[8] Πότερον ἐπιστήμην τὸ ἀγαθὸν φῂς εἶναι, ἢ ἡδονήν, ἢ ὃ ἄλλ τι παρὰ ταῦτα, p. 506 [B].

Concerning ΤΟ ΑΓΑΘΟΝ.

p. 99 [c].
Plato, in the *Phædo*, makes Socrates, in discussing the doctrine of Anaxagoras, speak with disapprobation of his not referring things to goodness and fitness as their causes: ὡς ἀληθῶς τὸ ἀγαθὸν καὶ δέον ξυνδεῖν καὶ ξυνέχειν οὐδὲν οἴονται. Here δέον, and of course τὸ ἀγαθόν, to which Socrates would refer the composition and support of things, must be the final cause. If any doubt of this could remain, it would be completely dispelled by a reference to what Socrates said in the preceding page he expected from the profession of Anaxagoras. 'When', says he, 'Anaxagoras professed that things were disposed by mind, I never imagined that he would assign any other cause for them than this, that it is best they should be in the manner in which they are'[9].

I will endeavour to throw some light upon this subject from the works of contemporary writers. 33

Xenophon was a scholar of Socrates at the same time with Plato, and has also handed down to posterity many of the discourses of that great teacher of morality to the Gentiles. Not being, like Plato, the founder of a sect and a lecturer by profession, he did not study to form an ingenious system with materials, culled with the nicest art from the traditions of diverse countries and the speculations of diverse masters. He told his artless tale with an unaffected though elegant simplicity.

---

[9] Οὐ γὰρ ἄν ποτε αὐτὸν ᾤμην, φάσκοντά γε ὑπὸ νοῦ αὐτὰ κεκοσμῆσθαι, ἄλλην τινα αὐτοῖς αἰτίαν ἐπενεγκεῖν, ἢ ὅτι βέλτιστον αὐτὰ οὕτως ἔχειν ἐστίν, ὥσπερ ἔχει.

[10] Εἴ τι εἰδείη ἀγαθόν: [i.e. if he knew of any thing good.]

Concerning TO ΑΓΑΘΟΝ.

It is not wonderful that the discourses of Socrates should appear different in the hands of such different relators. One of the most striking points of distinction is this, that in Xenophon Socrates always leads those who dispute with him from abstract and general reasonings to particulars.

It happens that he has preserved a discourse between Socrates and Aristippus concerning the very subject of which we have been treating. As Xenophon is supposed not to have been on the most friendly terms with Plato, I cannot help thinking that by a particular expression he meant to cast some ridicule upon this doctrine of our author, which Aristotle likewise seems to have thought very open to reprehension from the frequent strictures which he has passed upon it.

34 Xenophon tells us that Aristippus, desirous of ensnaring Socrates, asked him if he knew what good is[10]? Do you mean, says Socrates, good for a fever? No. For weakness of eyes? No. For hunger? No. Then, says he, if you ask me whether I know anything good, that is good for nothing, I neither know nor desire it[11]. He then proceeded to shew that there was nothing absolutely and universally good; for that good referred to some end; and things that were handsome and good for some purposes, were unseemly and bad for others.

Aristotle begins his *Ethics* with asserting that

Memorab. iii. 8. [§ 1.]

---

11 Ἆρα γὰρ [leg. γε] ἔφη, ἐρωτᾷς με, εἴ τι οἶδα πυρετοῦ ἀγαθόν; οὐκ ἔγωγ᾽, ἔφη. ἀλλ᾽ ὀφθαλμίας; οὐδὲ τοῦτο. ἀλλὰ λιμοῦ; οὐδὲ λιμοῦ. ἀλλὰ μὴν, ἔφη, εἴγ᾽ ἐρωτᾷς με, εἴ τι ἀγαθὸν οἶδα, ὃ μηδένος ἀγαθόν ἐστιν, οὔτ᾽ οἶδα, ἔφη, οὔτε δέομαι.

some good is the object of all our aims and pursuits; therefore that which all things desire is called good in an absolute sense, or The Good [12]. This in the second chapter he farther styles happiness. But here he gives us the same account that we have seen before in Plato and Cicero. Men doubt about the nature of this happiness [13]. The many, (οἱ πολλοί), as Plato also calls them, think that it consists of external things—as pleasure, riches. Some were of opinion that there was something good in itself which was the cause to other things of their being good [14].

Having in the third chapter confuted the opinions of the multitude, he undertakes, in the fourth chapter, to controvert the latter opinion, which was entertained by those whom he denominates the wise. This he calls τὸ καθόλου and the opinion of some friends. He maintains that there can be no common or general idea of good (οὐκ ἂν εἴη κοίνη τις ἐπὶ τούτων ἰδέα), because good is expressed in so many different ways: in the subject, as in God and the soul; in the quality, as in the virtues; in the quantity, as in moderation, in time, and place, and so forth. Again, having distinguished good into ends and means (τὰ μὲν καθ' αὐτά, θάτερα δὲ διὰ ταῦτα) let us, says he, consider, if they be expressed according to one idea. The conclusion, which he draws from

---

[12] Πᾶσα τέχνη καὶ πᾶσα μεθόδος, ὁμοίως δὲ πρᾶξίς τε καὶ προαίρεσις ἀγαθοῦ τινος ἐφίεσθαι δοκεῖ. διὸ καλῶς ἀπεφήναντο τἀγαθὸν οὗ πάντα ἐφίεται. I. 1.

[13] Περὶ δὲ τῆς εὐδαιμονίας, τίς ἐστιν, ἀμφισβητοῦσι.

his reasoning, is, that there is not a common good according to one idea (οὐκ ἔστιν ἄρα τὸ ἀγαθὸν κοινόν τι κατὰ μίαν ἰδέαν). Thus Xenophon and Aristotle arrive at the same point by different roads. It appears most evident to me, that Aristotle throughout this whole chapter is controverting the doctrine of Plato concerning τὸ ἀγαθόν; and all his reasonings imply, that he understood his master to mean by it one general abstract idea of good, under which all other things intitled good are classed, which he calls κοινόν τι καθόλου καὶ ἕν, and again, ἕν τι τὸ κοινῇ κατηγορούμενον ἀγαθόν. Aristotle begins his *Great Morals* with an enquiry about the same τὸ ἀγαθόν, which he pronounces to be the end of all knowledge and power (πάσης ἐπιστήμης καὶ δυνάμεως ἐστί τι τέλος), and says, that the idea of good is that by partaking of which other things are good[15]. Having come to the same conclusion by nearly the same reasoning as before, he attacks Plato more closely for introducing such general and abstract speculations into political disquisitions. The profession of no particular art or science comprehends the knowledge of the good of every one. The physician knows not what is good in the art of a pilot, nor again the pilot what is good in the profession of a physician; but each knows and is con-

---

[14] Παρὰ τὰ πολλὰ ἀγαθὰ, ἄλλο τι καθ᾽ αὑτὸ εἶναι, ὃ καὶ τοῖσδε πᾶσιν αἴτιόν ἐστι τοῦ εἶναι ἀγαθά.

[15] Οὗ τἄλλα μετασχόντα ἀγαθά ἐστι· τοῦτο δ᾽ ἐστὶν ἡ ἰδέα τἀγαθοῦ.

cerned about the good of his own occupation. So neither does it concern politics to treat of a good which is common to all things. Wherefore, when any one undertakes to discourse of good, he ought not to speak of the idea. But the men, against whom this reasoning is directed, think, that they ought to treat of the idea; for they ought to treat of what is most completely good.—This, says he, can have no relation to politics, concerning which we are now speaking.—But perhaps the person professes to use this general good as a first principle, from which he will proceed to the particular good. But neither is this right; for he should use the principles peculiar to his subject (δεῖ τὰς ἀρχὰς οἰκείας λαμβάνειν). Otherwise he would resemble a man, who, in order to prove that the angles of a triangle are equal to two right angles, should begin with proving the soul immortal. Now we can prove the proposition, without proving the immortality of the soul; and in like manner we can speculate upon other goods, without the abstract universal idea of good (ἄνευ τοῦ κατὰ τὴν ἰδέαν ἀγαθοῦ). Therefore this is not the peculiar principle of that good which you are seeking.

Most of this reasoning is repeated in his *Ethics to Eudemus*, particularly that a general abstract good is of no use in politics[16]. He calls it likewise τὸ τοῦ ἀγαθοῦ εἶδος. And that you may not sup-

---

[16] Ὅτι μὲν οὖν οὐκ ἔστιν αὐτό τι ἀγαθόν, ἔχει ἀπορίας τοιαύτας, καὶ ὅτι οὐ χρήσιμον τῇ πολιτικῇ, ἀλλὰ ἴδιόν τι ἀγαθόν, ὥσπερ καὶ ταῖς ἄλλαις.

pose it different from other species or general ideas, he says, ὥστ᾽ εἶναι αὐτὸ τὸ ἀγαθὸν τὴν 38 ἰδέαν τοῦ ἀγαθοῦ· καὶ γὰρ χωριστὴν εἶναι τῶν μετεχόντων, ὥσπερ καὶ τὰς ἄλλας ἰδέας. I think, I have now said enough to prove that Plato did not intend by the term τὸ ἀγαθὸν to express a person, and therefore that he could not mean by it the supreme Being, the first person of the Trinity; but rather the final cause of things, as he says in the *Philebus*, τό γε μὴν οὗ ἕνεκα τὸ p. 54. ἕνεκά του γιγνόμενον ἀεὶ γίγνοιτ᾽ ἂν ἐν τῇ τοῦ ἀγαθοῦ μοίρᾳ ἐκεῖνο ἐστι. In the *Philebus*, in which Plato professedly treats of the same subject, he does not soar quite so high into the regions of abstraction. The question having been started, whether pleasure (ἡδονή) or intellect and knowledge (νοῦς καὶ ἐπιστήμη) are the greatest good; in the course of the enquiry he divides both pleasure and knowledge into two kinds, differing from each other in degrees of truth and reality; and concludes, that neither of them separately, but that a mixture of the most pure parts of each, constitutes that good which is the subject of enquiry.

17 Νῦν δή τις λόγος ἐμήνυσεν ἡμῖν, ὥσπερ καὶ κατ᾽ ἀρχὰς, μὴ ζητεῖν ἐν τῷ ἀμίκτῳ βίῳ τἀγαθὸν, ἀλλ᾽ ἐν τῷ μικτῷ, [p. 61 B.]—Εἰ τὰ ἀληθέστατα τμήματα ἑκατέρας ἴδοιμεν πρῶτον ξυμμίξαντες, ἆρα ἱκανὰ ταῦτα ξυγκεκραμένα τὸν ἀγαπητότατον βίον ἀπεργασάμενα παρέχειν ἡμῖν; p. 61 [E].

PHILEBUS.

p. 578. See also p. 591.

IN Cudworth's *Intellectual System* is the following passage: " In his *Philebus*, though he agree thus far with those other ancient philosophers, ὡς ἀεὶ τοῦ παντὸς νοῦς ἄρχει, 'that mind always rules over the whole universe"; yet does he add afterwards, ὅτι νοῦς ἐστι γενούστης τοῦ πάντων αἰτίου, 'that mind is' (not absolutely the first principle but) 'cognate with the cause of all things;' and that therefore it rules over all things with and in a kind of subordination to that first principle, which is *Tagathon*, or the highest good.—Where when Plato affirms, that mind or his second divine hypostasis is γενούστης with the first; it is all one as if he should have said, that it is συγγένης, and ὁμοείδης, and ὁμογένης with it; all which words are used by Athanasius as synonymous with ὁμοούσιος 'coessential' or 'consubstantial' ".

[p. 84 c.]

Plato often speaks of the authority which the mind or soul in general exercises over the body, which it animates and informs. He applies to them severally the epithets, governing and governed (ἄρχων καὶ ἀρχόμενον).—In the *Timæus*, speaking of the creation of the universe, he says, ' The soul, which was prior in time and superior in dignity, was appointed by the Creator as a mistress and governor over the subject body'[1]. Hence it is reasonable to suppose, that νοῦς, ὃς ἄρχει τοῦ παντός, is the mind of the universe (τοῦ παντός).—But, in order to arrive at the full meaning of the passage upon which Cudworth has given this commentary, it will be proper to consider the context, and to observe the train of reasoning that led to it.

A dispute had arisen between Philebus and Socrates, whether pleasure or intellect contributed most to the good of man. In the course of the enquiry Socrates divided all things now existing in the universe (πάντα τὰ νῦν ὄντα ἐν τῷ παντὶ) into four parts. First, what is *unlimited* (ἄπειρον) [p. 27 B.] viz. those things which admit of degrees, and have no principle of limitation within themselves, such as hard, soft, harder, softer, &c. Secondly, *limitation* (πέρας). Thirdly, things produced by the union of limitation with what is in its own nature unlimited (κοινόν). And fourthly, the author or cause of the union (τὸ τῆς αἰτίας γένος.)—Having proved that pleasure is of the kind of the unlimited, he then asks, To which of the forementioned divisions can we without impiety assign wisdom, and knowledge, and mind, or intellect? (φρόνησιν δὲ καὶ ἐπιστήμην καὶ νοῦν εἰς τί ποτε [p. 13 B.] τῶν προειρημένων νυν θέντες οὐκ ἂν ἀσεβοῖμεν;) or, as he asks the same question again in other words, Of what kind they are (νοῦν καὶ ἐπιστήμην [p. 28 c.] ἐρόμενος ὁποίου γένους εἶεν). This, says he, is

---

[1] Ὁ δὲ καὶ γενέσει καὶ ἀρετῇ προτέραν καὶ πρεσβυτέραν ψυχὴν σώματος, ὡς δεσπότιν καὶ ἄρξουσαν ἀρξομένου συνεστήσατο.

easy; for all wise men agree, that mind is king of heaven and earth. And perhaps they say well. But let us, if you please, enter into an examination of the kind itself (αὐτοῦ τοῦ γένους) more at large.

[p. 28 D.] Shall we, says he, assert that an irrational power and chance preside over the universe; or on the contrary, as those who have gone before us say, that some wonderful mind and intelligence arranges and directs it? (νοῦν καὶ φρόνησίν τινα θαυμαστὴν συντάττουσαν διακυβερνᾶν;) Protarchus, one of his opponents, readily admits that mind disposes all things (νοῦν πάντα διακοσμεῖν). Socrates encourages him to persist in this opinion, and assures him that he will take his share of the danger and censure, if any doughty disputant should affirm that those things were not so disposed, but proceeded in a disorderly manner (ὅταν ἀνὴρ δεινὸς [p. 29 A.] φῇ ταῦτα μὴ οὕτως ἀλλ' ἀτάκτως ἔχειν).

He then states the constituent parts of the visible world and human nature. The fire with which we are conversant, is supplied and replenished by the elemental fire which subsists in the universe 42 (ἐν τῷ παντί) in a perfect state. It must be said also of our bodies that they proceed from and are supported by the great body of the Universe. Do we not say that our body has a soul[2]? Whence

---

[2] See this reasoning adopted in Cic. *De Nat. Deor.* II. 6, 7.

[3] We find an argument similar to this both in Xenophon and Cicero. Νοῦν δὲ μόνον ἄρα οὐδαμοῦ ὄντα σὲ εὐτυχῶς πως δοκεῖς συναρπάσαι; καὶ τάδε τὰ ὑπερμεγέθη καὶ πλῆθος ἄπειρα δι' ἀφροσύνην τινα, ὡς οἴει, εὐτάκτως ἔχειν;— Xen. *Memorab.* I. 4. [§ 8].

PHILEBUS. 39

did it receive it, if the body of the universe be not animated, and have the same things as this of ours, and still more beautiful? There are, therefore, in the universe a kind, unlimited limitation, and some cause, not unimportant, presiding over them (ἄπει- [p. 30 c.] ρον, πέρας, καί τις ἐπ' αὐτοῖς αἰτία οὐ φαύλη) arranging and constituting years, seasons, and months, which is most justly called wisdom, and mind, or intellect[3]. But wisdom and intellect cannot subsist without soul[4]. Therefore, we must acknowledge that there is in the nature of Jupiter (that is, the universe) a royal soul, and a royal mind, on account of the power of the cause. Think not, says Socrates, that I have produced this reasoning to no purpose. It supports those who said of old that mind always governs the world. It also furnishes this answer to my enquiry, That mind is of the same kind with the cause of all things.

It is evident, first, that the following passages all mean the same thing, viz., Νοῦς ἐστὶ βασιλεὺς ἡμῖν οὐρανοῦ καὶ γῆς—Νοῦν καὶ φρόνησίν τινα θαυμαστὴν συντάττουσαν διακυβερνᾶν—Νοῦν πάντα διακοσμεῖν—Ἀεὶ τοῦ παντὸς νοῦς ἄρχει; and that they are put in opposition to the following sentences; Τὰ [p. 28 d.] ξύμπαντα καὶ τόδε τὸ καλούμενον ὅλον ἐπιτροπεύειν τὴν τοῦ ἀλόγου καὶ εἰκῆ δύναμιν, καὶ τὰ ὅπη ἔτυχεν, and Ἀτάκτως ἔχειν. Secondly, that the two

---

Quid est enim verius, quam neminem esse oportere tam stulto arrogantem, ut in se rationem et mentem putet inesse, in coelo mundoque non putet?—Cic. de Leg. II. 7.

[4] Philo says, that intellect (νοῦς) is to the soul what the pupil is to the eye. Ψυχῇ τινα ψυχὴν καθάπερ κόρην ἐν ὀφθαλμῷ. Περὶ Κοσμοποιίας, p. 14.

following passages express, and the third refers, to the same question: Φρόνησιν δὲ καὶ ἐπιστήμην καὶ νοῦν εἰς τί ποτε τῶν προειρημένων νῦν θέντες, οὐκ ἀσεβοῖμεν ;—Νοῦν καὶ ἐπιστήμην ἐρόμενος ὁποίου γένους εἶεν—Διὰ μακροτέρων δ᾽, εἰ βούλει, τὴν σκέψιν αὐτοῦ τοῦ γένους ποιησώμεθα—And that the answer to this question is, Νοῦς ἐστὶ γενούστης τοῦ πάντων αἰτίου λεχθέντος τῶν τεττάρων, ὧν ἦν ἡμῖν ἓν τοῦτο. As Socrates himself immediately after expresses in direct terms, ἔχεις γὰρ δήπου νῦν ἡμῶν ἤδη τὴν ἀπόκρισιν. Thirdly, that Νοῦς, which is said to be γενούστης τοῦ πάντων αἰτίου, of the same kind or akin to the cause of all things is the human mind or intellect considered as a source of good in opposition to pleasure (ἡδονή), which, consisting of sensations, was stated to be of the kind of unlimited (ἄπειρον). For Socrates proceeds thus : It has now been satisfactorily shewn by us of what kind it is, and of what power it is possessed (οὗ μὲν γένους ἐστὶ καὶ τίνα ποτὲ δύναμιν κέκτηται) ; and also the kind (γένος) of pleasure in like manner some time ago appeared. He then repeats the result of the preceding investigation : 'We should remember these things concerning both ; that mind is akin to the cause, and in a manner of the same kind with it (νοῦς μὲν αἰτίας ἦν ξυγγενὴς καὶ τούτου σχεδὸν τοῦ γένους) ; but pleasure is itself unlimited, and of a kind that neither has nor ever will have in and of itself, either beginning, or middle, or end.'

This doctrine, that the soul of man is akin to the soul of the universe and derived from it, appears frequently in the writings of Plato and his followers. In the tenth book of his *Republic*, he characterizes it as related to the divine and immortal, and always existing (ὡς συγγενὴς οὖσα τῷ τε θείῳ καὶ ἀθανάτῳ καὶ ἀεὶ ὄντι). It abounds everywhere in Cicero: *Quod prævideat animus per se, quippe qui Deorum cognatione teneatur.* De Divin. I. 30: *Necesse est cognatione divinorum animorum animos humanos commoveri,* 49. When we consider how copiously Cicero drew his materials from Plato, and what a variety of passages, almost literally translated, he has transfused into his works; it is not unreasonable to suspect that he had our author and his doctrine immediately in his eye when he wrote the following part of his Treatise concerning *Laws: Cumque alia, quibus cohærent homines, e mortali genere sumserint, quæ fragilia essent et caduca; animum esse ingeneratum a Deo: ex quo vere vel agnatio nobis cum cœlestibus vel genus vel stirps appellari potest. Jam vero virtus eadem in homine ac deo est, neque ullo alio ingenio præterea: est autem virtus nihil aliud quam in se perfecta et ad summum perducta natura. Est igitur homini cum Deo similitudo. Quod cum ita sit, quæ tandem potest esse prior certiorve cognatio?*

Moreover, both Cicero, and Maximus Tyrius, another professed admirer and follower of Plato, have applied this very doctrine of the human mind's being derived from the divine, as an argument to prove the very same point for which Plato has here produced it, viz., the superior efficacy of intellect above sensual pleasure to promote the real good of man. Cicero prefaces his reasoning with

42 PHILEBUS.

[*Tusculanæ Disput.* Lib. v. cap. 12. § 87.]

an immediate reference to Plato: *Ex hoc igitur Platonis quasi quodam sancto augustoque fonte nostra omnis manabit oratio.* Having spoken of the nature and origin of vegetables and irrational animals, he next proceeds to man, the proper subject of his en-

[*Ibid.* cap. xiii. § 37.]

quiry. *Ut bestiis aliud alii præcipui a natura datum est, quod suum quæque retinet nec discedit ab eo; sic homini multo quiddam præstantius: etsi præstantia debent ea dici, quæ habent aliquam comparationem: humanus autem animus, decerptus ex mente divina, cum alio nullo, nisi cum ipso deo, si hoc fas est dictu, comparari potest. Hic igitur, si est excultus, et si ejus acies ita curata est, ut ne cæcetur erroribus, fit perfecta mens, id est, absoluta ratio, quod est idem virtus. Et si omne beatum est, cui nihil deest, et quod in suo genere expletum atque cumulatum est idque virtutis est proprium: certe omnes, virtutis compotes, beati sunt.*

The passage in Maximus Tyrius stands thus:—
Ἔχει μὲν γὰρ, ἔχει νοῦν καὶ λόγον—καὶ παρὰ μὲν θνητῆς πλημμελείας τὸ σῶμα ἔχοντι, ἐκ δὲ τῆς ἀθανάτου ἀπορροῆς τὸν νοῦν διαλαμβάνοντι—ἴδιον δὲ σαρκῶν μὲν ἡδοναὶ, νοῦ δὲ λόγος—ἐνταῦθα τοίνυν ζήτει τὸ ἀνθρώπου ἀγαθὸν, ὅπου τὸ ἔργον—ἐνταῦθα τὸ ἔργον, ὅπου τὸ ὄργανον· ἐνταῦθα τὸ ὄργανον, ὅπου τὸ σῶζον—τί ψυχῆς ὄργανον; νοῦς. ζήτει τὸ ἔργον· τί νοῦ ἔργον; φρόνησις· εὗρες τὸ ἀγαθόν. *Dissert.* XXXIV.

EPISTLES.

THE SECOND EPISTLE TO *DIONYSIUS*.

THE reasoning and expression used in the *Philebus* will serve to throw some light upon a passage in the second *Epistle* to Dionysius: Φῂς [p. 312 D.] γὰρ δὴ κατὰ τὸν ἐκείνου λόγον, οὐχ ἱκανῶς ἀποδεδεῖχθαί σοι περὶ τῆς τοῦ πρώτου φύσεως. Φραστέον δή σοι δι' αἰνιγμῶν—ὧδε γὰρ ἔχει· περὶ τὸν πάντων βασιλέα πάντ' ἐστὶ καὶ ἐκείνου ἕνεκα πάντα· καὶ ἐκεῖνο αἴτιον ἁπάντων τῶν καλῶν. δεύτερον δὲ περὶ τὰ δεύτερα καὶ τρίτον περὶ τὰ τρίτα.

When we consider the character of Dionysius, and call to mind that the [1]purpose of Plato's visiting him was to inculcate moderation upon him; it is natural to suppose, that the reasoning used in the *Philebus*, would constitute a very important part of the Lectures delivered by the Philosopher to the Prince. He would state to him that there are in the universe three principles, ἄπειρον, πέρας, καὶ τὸ τῆς αἰτίας γένος: and as in the universe the most noble and beautiful productions are formed by the operation of mind or intellect connecting limitation,

---

[1] Plato explains this purpose in his seventh *Epistle*, which was directed to the friends of Dio. He says, that Dio, having attached himself to virtue in preference to pleasure and luxurious living (ἀρετὴν περὶ πλείονος ἡδονῆς τῆς τε ἄλλης τρυφῆς ἠγαπηκώς, p. 327 [B]), was desirous that Dionysius also should be brought to the same state of mind. He therefore prevailed upon Plato to make a voyage to Syracuse for that purpose.

with the things that are in themselves unlimited; so also in man the greatest good is produced by connecting limitation (πέρας) with the pleasing sensations (ἡδοναί) which are in their own nature unlimited.

We might likewise expect to find, that as long as the prince thought proper to continue the connection with the philosopher, this subject would engage a considerable part of their attention.

The passage in question confirms this reasoning, and is illustrated by it; though it is designedly involved in obscurity, that, in the case of the letter's miscarrying, it might not be understood by any but those who had some previous knowledge of the principles of the author. In it is contained an enumeration of the three principles; the first of which, τὸν πάντων βασιλέα, is the same as τὸ πάντων αἴτιον, βασιλεὺς ἡμῖν οὐρανοῦ καὶ γῆς, by which, from a mixture of the other two principles, ὡραί τε καὶ ὅσα ἄλλα πάντα ἡμῖν γέγονε, τῶν τε ἀπείρων καὶ τῶν πέρας ἐχόντων συμμιχθέντων.

[Philebus, p. 31 c.]

'The human mind,' proceeds Plato, 'is earnestly desirous of learning the nature of these things, looking into the things of itself that are related to them; none of which it has in a perfect state. But there is nothing of this kind (that is, of a state, which is not perfect) with respect to the king, and the things which I have mentioned: τοῦ δὴ βασιλέως πέρι καὶ ὧν εἶπον οὐδέν ἐστι τοιοῦτο. Consequently, the knowledge which the mind acquires of the nature τοῦ πρώτου, by looking into the corresponding things of itself, must be inadequate.'

[p. 313 A.]

Plato here alludes to what is taught in the *Philebus*; first, that the constituent parts of man are of the same kind with the constituent parts of the universe; secondly, that those parts in man are imperfect, but in the universe they are perfect.

The SIXTH EPISTLE.

[p. 323 D.] NEAR the latter end of Plato's sixth *Epistle* is the following passage: τὸν τῶν πάντων θεὸν, ἡγεμόνα τῶν τε ὄντων καὶ τῶν μελλόντων, τοῦ τε ἡγεμόνος καὶ αἰτίου πατέρα κύριον. The author here appears to me to express himself according to the system of a creator and a creation. I conceive, that τὸν πάντων Θεόν corresponds with τὸ πάντων αἴτιον and βασιλεὺς ἡμῖν κ. τ. λ. in the *Philebus*, the universe or the soul of the universe. According to this interpretation αἰτίου πατέρα κύριον must mean the eternal, self-existent being, the Creator of the universe, who is called in the *Timæus* δημιουργὸς and πατήρ.

CRATYLUS.

THE same terms in the *Philebus* are likewise explanatory of the following passages in the *Cratylus:* Οὐ γάρ ἐστιν ἡμῖν καὶ τοῖς ἄλλοις πᾶσιν, [p. 396 A.] ὅστις ἐστὶν αἴτιος μᾶλλον τοῦ ζῆν, ἢ ὁ ἄρχων τε καὶ βασιλεὺς τῶν πάντων. συμβαίνει οὖν ὀρθῶς ὀνομάζεσθαι οὕτως (Ζῆνα) τῷ θεὸς εἶναι, δι' ὃν ζῆν ἀεὶ πᾶσι τοῖς ζῶσιν ὑπάρχει. Cudworth saw the necessity of referring here to ψυχή[1], the third hypostasis of his Platonic Trinity, those very titles, which in other passages he supposes to be applied as distinguishing characteristics to the two other hypostases. But the truth is that they all refer to that one principle of life and intelligence, which was supposed to pervade the universe, and regulate all its motions and operations.

[1] Hanc ego mallem interpretationem junioribus, a quibus profecta est, Platonicis, Plotino et ceteris reliquisset vir doctissimus, quam suam fecisset. Nec enim, quamvis Plato Saturni, Jovis et Cœli loco isto mentionem faciat, ullum ego ibi vestigium video trium illorum principiorum, multo minus cum tribus his Platonicorum principiis tria Græcorum nomina componi cerno. Pessimi, meo judicio, Platonis interpretes sunt, qui post natum Servatorem Platonicorum adoptarunt sibi vocabulum. Quorum quidem animi, quoniam tribus illis principiis toti orant infecti et imbuti, ideo ubivis ea quoque sagacius, quam fas erat, in Platone venabantur, cujus quippe præcepta videri volebant unice inculcare.—Moshem. *in loc.* Tom. I. p. 380.

TIMÆUS.

THE *Timæus* of Plato cuts so distinguished a figure in the present question, and has been so often quoted and referred to by authors, that we may venture to enter upon an examination of it without any further preface.

[p. 27 D.] Timæus, who is the supposed expositor of the system advanced in this Dialogue, divides things into two classes. First, what is without beginning and unchangeable, which is comprehended by the understanding with reasoning. Secondly, what is made, and perishes, and is the subject of opinion only, being in its nature variable, and having nothing in it so stable, as to furnish the materials of knowledge properly so called.

What is made, necessarily implies an author. Now whatever the Creator forms, looking at what is invariable and using such a pattern, must be completely beautiful. But whatever he forms, looking at what has been made and using such a pattern, will not be completely beautiful.

Having considered the universe, and concluded from its being visible, that it was made; he next enquires whether the Creator in forming it looked at an invariable pattern, or at one that was made, and asserts, it is manifest, from the beauty of the work and the excellence of the Creator, that he looked at what is unchangeable. For, says he, *that is the most beautiful of the things which have been made, and he is the best of causes.* Thus it was formed according to a pattern, comprehensible by reason and thought, and unvarying. Having thus distinguished the image and the pattern, he states the nature of the account which he is about to give. He calls it only a probable story and probable reasonings (εἰκότα μῦθον καὶ εἰκότας λόγους) which they must be content, on account of the imperfection of their common nature, to accept, instead of such expositions as would correspond with the dignity of the subject. These latter, in opposition to the others, he calls αὐτοῖς ὁμολογουμένους καὶ ἀπηκριβωμένους λόγους. [p. 29 c.] He then proceeds to inquire into the reason and manner of the creation. The first he attributes to the goodness of the Creator. With respect to the manner, he says, the Creator took what is visible, viz. matter[1], which moved irregularly and disorderly, and reduced it to order from disorder, on account of the excellence of the former above the latter.

He considered also (λογισάμενος) that what is intelligent is more excellent than what is devoid of intelligence; but that there cannot be mind or intelligence without soul or life. On account of this reasoning (διὰ τὸν λογισμὸν τόνδε) having constituted a mind in a soul and a soul in a body,

[p. 29 c.]
[p. 30 b.]
[p. 29 c.]
[p. 30 b.]

---

[1] Ἀλλὰ καὶ τούτου [l. τούτῳ] πάλιν ὁ μεγαλόφωνος Πλάτων οὐχ ὁμολογεῖ, λέγων ἀρχὰς εἶναι Θεὸν, καὶ ὕλην καὶ παράδειγμα.—Hermiæ *Irrisio Gentil. Philosoph.* [c. xi. p. 221].

he composed the whole, that he might complete a work most beautiful and excellent in its nature. Thus ought we to say, according to a probable account (κατὰ λόγον τὸν εἰκότα) that this world was in truth made an animated and intelligent being by the Providence of God (διὰ τὴν τοῦ Θεοῦ γενέσθαι πρόνοιαν). The whole composition of the soul, he says, was completed according to the mind of the composer (κατὰ νοῦν ξυνιστάντι).

[p. 88 c.] When he speaks afterwards of the production of time, in which this animated and intelligent being should exist, he says, Therefore from such reasoning and consideration of God (ἐξ οὖν λόγου καὶ διανοίας Θεοῦ τοιαύτης) the sun, &c. was made.

From all this it appears most evident to me, that λογισμός, πρόνοια, λόγος, and διάνοια Θεοῦ are only operations of the supreme intelligence, as p. 44 [c]. προνοίας θεῶν is of the inferior gods.

I will now examine the nature of the pattern and the image spoken of in this discourse.

I have already shewn at large, that, in the writings of Plato, general or abstract ideas are considered as the real entities, on account of the stability of their nature, different from particular existences, which are in a state of perpetual change; and that he denominated them ever-existing, as they bear no relation to time, nor are they affected by it. I will, however, produce a passage or two more to confirm a point of so much importance in determining the meaning of the pattern mentioned in the *Timæus*, a misconception

TIMÆUS. 51

concerning which has been very extensive in its operation.

It is one of the leading principles of the Platonic Philosophy, that general or abstract ideas only can be the foundation of real knowledge; as they only are exact and permanent in their nature and relations².

56 The *Timæus* of Plato is derived from the treatise of Timæus the Locrian, concerning the soul of the world. In this treatise the pattern (παρά- [p. 93 b.] δειγμα) is called ἰδέα and εἶδος, the *idea* and the *specific form*, which was eternal and co-existent with ὕλη, matter, but distinct from and opposite

² Arguing upon this principle in his Dialogue concerning a *Republic*, (Lib. v. [p. 479 A]), he reprobates the pretensions to wisdom advanced in favour of those men, who are conversant with particulars only. Ἀποκρινέσθω ὁ χρηστός, ὃς αὐτὸ μὲν κάλον καὶ ἰδέαν τινὰ αὐτοῦ κάλλους μηδεμίαν ἡγεῖται ἀεὶ κατὰ ταὐτὰ ὡσαύτως ἔχουσαν· πολλὰ δὲ τὰ καλὰ νομίζει ἐκεῖνος ὁ φιλοθεάμων, καὶ οὐδαμῇ ἀνεχόμενος, ἄν τις ἓν τὸ καλὸν φῇ εἶναι καὶ δίκαιον καὶ τἆλλα οὕτω. True philosophers he characterizes thus, [p. 479 E]: τοὺς αὐτὰ ἕκαστα θεωμένους καὶ ἀεὶ κατὰ τὰ αὐτὰ ὡσαύτως ὄντα. Again, in the beginning of the following book, he defines philosophers, [p. 484 A], οἱ τοῦ ἀεὶ κατὰ ταὐτὰ ὡσαύτως ἔχοντος δυνάμενοι ἐφάπτεσθαι. The terms in which he describes the unphilosophic, deserve our particular attention : τοῦ ὄντος ἑκάστου ἐστερημένοι τῆς γνώσεως, καὶ μηδὲν ἐναργὲς ἐν τῇ ψυχῇ ἔχοντες παράδειγμα. Again, (p. 486 [D]), speaking of the turn of mind to be expected in a philosopher, he says, ἔμμετρον ἄρα καὶ εὔχαριν ζητῶμεν πρὸς τοῖς ἄλλοις διάνοιαν φύσει, ἣν ἐπὶ τὴν τοῦ ὄντος ἰδέαν ἑκάστου τὸ αὐτοφυὲς εὐάγωγον παρέξει. By the two last cited passages it appears, that the terms ἰδέα and παράδειγμα are used to express abstract ideas. Agreeable to this is the account which Diogenes Laertius gives of the philosophy of Plato: Ἔστι δὲ τῶν εἰδῶν ἓν ἕκαστον ἀΐδιόν τε καὶ νόημα, καὶ πρὸς τούτοις ἀπαθές· διὸ καί φησιν ἐν τῇ φύσει τὰς ἰδέας ἑστάναι καθάπερ παραδείγματα· τὰ δ' ἄλλα ταύταις ἐοικέναι, τούτων ὁμοιώματα καθεστῶτα. [Lib. iii. Segm. 13].

to it. What was formed at the creation by the conjunction of these two, is called their offspring (τὰ ἐκ τούτων ἔκγονα). Information concerning these three is attained by three different ways—concerning idea or specific form, by the mind according to knowledge—concerning elemental matter, by spurious reasoning (λογισμῷ νόθῳ), so called, because it does not arrive at that certainty and precision which are attained by abstract reasoning—concerning their offspring, particular material objects, produced by the union of specific form with elemental matter, by sensation and opinion.

[p. 94 B.]

[p. 94 C.]

We are to understand, says the philosopher, that, before the creation, there were Idea or abstract form, Matter, and God the Creator. Now God saw matter assuming specific form (τὴν ἰδέαν) and changing, in all ways indeed, but disorderly. He was therefore desirous of bringing it to order, of converting it from its indeterminate state, and of making it determinate—that there might be distinctions of bodies, and that they might not receive undirected changes.

57

Let us now consider Plato's description of the pattern. He says that it contained within itself all intelligible animals; as this world contains us and all other living creatures. For God, desiring to make this world resemble, as much as possible, the most beautiful of intelligibles which was in all respects perfect, made it one visible animal, having within it all corresponding animals, according to its nature. If due allowance be made for the peculiar language of the Pythagorean and Platonic schools, nothing can be more plain than that the pattern signifies no more than the abstract idea, according to which the universe was formed, with parts in the one answering to parts in the other [3].

Aristotle distinguishes the causes of things into four kinds: First, the subject matter, as brass in the composition of a statue, &c. Secondly, the specific or generic form. Thirdly, the author. Fourthly, the final cause. The terms in which he describes the second kind, or specific and generic forms, are these, τὸ εἶδος καὶ τὸ παράδειγμα· τοῦτο δ' ἐστὶν ὁ λόγος ὁ τοῦ τί ἦν εἶναι καὶ τὰ τούτου γένη. *Natur. Ausc.* ii. 3.

With respect to the nature of the soul of the universe, it may be proper, first, to observe that mind and soul do not signify two distinct independent existences, as some have supposed. Ψυχὴ, *soul*, when considered separately, signifies the principle of life: Νοῦς, *mind*, the principle of intelligence. Or, according to Plutarch, soul is the cause and beginning of motion, and mind of order and harmony with respect to motion [4]. Together they signify an intelligent soul (ἔννους ψυχὴ) which is sometimes called a rational soul (ψυχὴ λογική). Hence, when the nature of the soul is not in question, the word ψυχὴ is used to express both. Thus *Plat. Quæst.* p. 1015 [B].

[3] Νοητὸς ἐπάγῃ κόσμος τὸ τοῦ φαινομένου τοῦδε ἀρχέτυπον, ἰδέαις ἀοράτοις συσταθεὶς ὥσπερ οὗτος σώμασιν ὁρατοῖς.—Philo Judæus, *De Confus. Ling.* p. 345.

[4] Ψυχὴ γὰρ αἰτία κινήσεως καὶ ἀρχή, νοῦς δὲ τάξεως καὶ συμφωνίας περὶ κίνησιν.

in the *Phædo* the soul (ψυχή) is said sometimes to use the body for the examination of things (τῷ σώματι προσχρῆται εἰς τὸ σκοπεῖν τι); at which times, according to the principles of Plato, it forms confused and imperfect notions of things, and is involved in error. But, when it examines things by itself, it arrives at what is pure and always existing and immortal and uniform, and is free from error. Here the highest operations of νοῦς, 'mind,' are indisputably attributed to ψυχὴ, 'soul.'

Aristotle, describing ψυχὴ, 'soul,' says, that during anger, confidence, desire, &c. it participates with the body; but that the act of understanding belongs peculiarly to itself[5]. Again, he says, Plato in the *Timæus*, in the same manner as Empedocles, makes the soul out of the elemental principles of things; for that like is known by like[6]. Soon after he says, that soul has in it a principle both of motion and of knowledge[7].

It is evident, that πᾶν τόδε or κόσμος, here treated of by Plato, is the system of heaven and earth, and of the several natures contained in them[8]. And that νοῦς καὶ ψυχὴ κόσμου is, as Cicero expresses it, *vis quædam sentiens, quæ est toto confusa mundo*, performing the same functions in the great body of the universe at large, that human souls do in our bodies, giving life and motion to its several

---

[5] Φαίνεται δὲ τῶν πλείστων οὐθὲν ἄνευ σώματος πάσχειν οὐδὲ ποιεῖν, οἷον ὀργίζεσθαι, θαρρεῖν, ἐπιθυμεῖν, ὅλως αἰσθάνεσθαι. μάλιστα δ' ἔοικεν ἴδιον τὸ νοεῖν. Περὶ Ψυχῆς, Lib. I. cap. 1.

[6] Τὸν αὐτὸν τρόπον ἐν τῷ Τιμαίῳ Πλάτων τὴν ψυχὴν ἐκ τῶν στοιχείων ποιεῖ· γιγνώσκεσθαι γὰρ ὁμοίῳ ὅμοιον. cap. 11.

parts, directing those motions with consummate wisdom, and communicating different portions of its essence to the different beings that are contained within the bounds of its all-comprehending circumference; thus effecting and maintaining the variations of times and of seasons, the changes of organized and unorganized matter, and the uninterrupted succession of animated and rational beings. The proof of the existence of this rational soul, animating and directing the universe, was derived, as has been already observed, from the observable fecundity of nature, and the order and harmony of its parts and motions.

That πᾶν τόδε or κόσμος was not eternal *a parte ante* is manifest from the whole tenor of the relation. We have the reasoning of the Creator concerning this future God, before he was created (λογισμὸς θεοῦ περὶ τὸν ἐσόμενον θεόν). We have a [p. 34 B.] direct assertion of the creation of it: διὰ δὴ τὸν [p. 80 B.] λογισμὸν τόνδε, νοῦν μὲν ἐν ψυχῇ, ψυχὴν δὲ ἐν σώματι συνιστάς, τὸ πᾶν ξυνετεκταίνετο: on account of this reasoning having constituted a mind in a soul and a soul in a body, he composed the whole. Thus this world was made by the providence of God an animated and intelligent being (ζῶον ἔμψυχον ἔννουν τε).

Nay, the philosopher does not even stop here,

---

7 Ἐπεὶ δὲ καὶ κινητικὸν ἐδόκει ἡ ψυχὴ εἶναι καὶ γνωριστικόν. *Ibid.*

8 Κόσμος μὲν οὖν ἐστὶ σύστημα ἐξ οὐρανοῦ καὶ γῆς καὶ τῶν ἐν τούτοις περιεχομένων φύσεων.—Aristot. Περὶ Κόσμου, Cap. 1.

Δῆλος γὰρ ὁ λογιζόμενος θεὸς ὁ δημιουργός· ὁ δὲ ἐσόμενος καὶ γιγνόμενος αἰεὶ ὁ κόσμος.—Stobæi *Ecl. Phy.* I. [2. § 28.]

but lays before us the order of the work and the particulars of the composition; the result of which is contained in the following words: διὰ πάντα δὴ ταῦτα εὐδαίμονα θεὸν αὐτὸν ἐγεννήσατο. Time is said to have been made with it; that, having been made together, they might also be dissolved together, if there should ever be a dissolution of them (ἵνα ἅμα γεννηθέντες ἅμα καὶ λυθῶσιν, ἄν ποτε λύσις αὐτῶν γένηται). That it is not incapable of being dissolved is clear from the declaration of the Creator to the Gods, whom he styles θεοὶ θεῶν: 'every thing that has been compacted is dissoluble. Wherefore since you have been made you are not immortal (τὸ μὲν οὖν δὴ δεθὲν πᾶν λυτόν—δι' ἃ καὶ ἐπείπερ γεγένησθε, ἀθάνατοι μὲν οὐκ ἐστέ).' It is manifest, likewise, from the terms in which τὸ πᾶν, the universe itself, is described in the treatise of Timæus the Locrian: τοῦτον ἐποίη θεὸν γεννατόν, οὔποκα φθαρησόμενον ὑπ' ἄλλῳ αἰτίῳ, ἔξω τῶ αὐτὸν συντεταγμένῳ θέω, εἴποκα δήλετο αὐτὸν διαλύεν.

It will be proper to repeat here an observation, which was made at the beginning of the examination of the *Parmenides*. Plato in the *Timæus*, as well as in that Dialogue, is unwilling to make himself or Socrates responsible for the truth of the doctrines which are maintained in it. He therefore does not, according to his usual custom, advance them as the sentiments of Socrates; but attributes them to another for whose credit he is not so much concerned. He, moreover, does not pretend that the knowledge of them was attained by the principles of reason; but he founds their truth upon the authority of tradition.

62 This observation will serve to explain a circumstance which must otherwise appear very extraordinary. The real opinion of Plato concerning the eternity of the world has been much controverted at different periods of time. If the *Timæus* represented the genuine sentiments of Plato, it would be impossible for any rational doubts to be entertained upon the subject. For this Dialogue not only contains the most express declarations that the world had a beginning, but also explains the nature of the different parts of which it was composed; and states the order in which they were at first severally created and afterwards compacted. But if we consider him in this Dialogue as only representing the sentiments of another, without intending to pledge himself absolutely for the truth of them; nothing decisive and incontrovertible can be derived from this Dialogue for settling the controversy.

In this Dialogue the Creator, who existed eternally, is distinguished from the intelligent soul of the world, which, we are told, was actually created, though prior in time and superior in dignity to the body of gross matter which it animates and modifies. This intelligent soul is generally considered by the ancients as the principle and source of life and intelligence, and the supporter of order and harmony in the universe; and therefore in all ordinary cases
63 an investigation of the nature and origin of things usually terminates in it.

Minucius Felix informs us, that the God of Py- *Octavius*, cap. xix. [§ 7.]

thagoras was described in terms of the same import: *Pythagoræ Deus est animus, per universam rerum naturam commeans et intentus; ex quo etiam animalium omnium vita capiatur.*

Recourse was seldom had to any other being, except to account for the origin of the universe in opposition to those who maintained, that it existed from eternity. They, who asserted that the universe was created, were under the necessity of providing a Creator. But they seldom made any other use of him, than just to account for the origin of the world. Hence Plato excuses himself from enlarging upon the nature and attributes of this supreme Being, by saying that it is difficult to discover the Maker and Father of this universe; and when he has been discovered, it is impossible to declare him to all: Τὸν μὲν οὖν ποιητὴν καὶ πατέρα τοῦδε τοῦ παντὸς εὑρεῖν τε ἔργον καὶ εὑρόντα εἰς πάντας ἀδύνατον λέγειν. In this case, however, the soul of the world, the principle of life and intelligence, the supporter of the succession of beings, and the maintainer of order in the universe, held only the second place. Whereas, on the other hypothesis, this same principle is held to be the first cause.

What Origen says of the Stoics and Platonics is perfectly agreeable to this: the Greeks affirm that the whole world is a God: the Stoics that it is the first God: the Platonics that it is the second[9].

---

[9] Σαφῶς δὴ τὸν ὅλον κόσμον λέγουσιν εἶναι θεὸν, Στωϊκοὶ μὲν τὸν πρῶτον· οἱ δ' ἀπὸ Πλάτωνος τὸν δεύτερον.—*Contra Celsum*, Lib. v. p. 235.

The Stoics maintained the eternity of the world. They had therefore occasion to account for no more than the succession of beings, and the wisdom and order with which the affairs of the universe were conducted. For this the soul of the world was sufficient, and was esteemed their first God. The Platonics derived most of their opinions from the *Timæus*, in which the doctrine of a Creator is taught. He therefore was necessarily the first God; and the soul of the world could occupy only the second place of dignity in this system. An attention to this distinction will serve to account for that apparent inconsistency in the principles of Plato, to which Cicero makes Velleius the Stoic object. [De Nat. Deor. Lib. i. cap. 12.]

It would be easy to produce a great number of instances from the writings of Plato, Cicero, and others, in support of what is here laid down. But, as on any supposition it is equally impossible to discover in this Dialogue the doctrine of the Holy Trinity; it would lead me too far from the immediate subject of my enquiry to dwell any longer upon this topic. For the same reason, because I would not meddle with anything that is not immediately and necessarily connected with my subject, I have declined entering into the controversy concerning Plato's opinion of the nature and mode of the subsistence of ideas. Whether it be determined that Plato taught that they subsisted notionally or substantially in the divine intellect; the decision, I conceive, will not of itself tend in the slightest degree to prove Plato's doctrine to have been, that the intellect is personally distinct from the Supreme Being, to whom it belongs. Still less, if possible, can the question be affected by any other hypothesis concerning the nature and mode of the subsistence of ideas.

Having examined all the principal passages, which are produced from the writings of Plato, to prove that he was acquainted with the doctrine of three hypostases in the divine nature; and having shewn, as I conceive, that none of them, in their true and genuine signification, do actually countenance the hypothesis; I will endeavour to investigate the subject farther, and trace out the origin and progress of the opinion in later times.

SEVERAL sects of Pagan Philosophy in a manner derived their origin from the school of Plato, yet no one of them, whether it professed to adopt his opinions in the whole, or only in part, either affirmed or denied this article, which, if it had been really maintained by Plato, must have held so distinguished a place among his tenets. Even Cicero has taken no notice of this striking peculiarity; though he not only was a passionate admirer and imitator of Plato, but also made it the chief employment of his latter days to transpose into the Roman language the most important doctrines and reasonings of the several sects of Grecian Philosophy. This profound silence is too remarkable and too general to be attributed to chance. Neither the high estimation in which the writings of Plato were held, nor the penetration and industry of the many learned men, who either propagated or avowedly deviated from his opinions, will permit us for a moment to suppose that this article could have been wholly overlooked, or regarded as a circumstance of no moment.

67 If this opinion cannot be found in the writings of Plato, and is not attributed to him by the subsequent philosophers of Greece and Rome, it is of

importance to investigate, by what means it gained admission among men. For this purpose it will be necessary to examine at large the writings of Philo, an Hellenist Jew, who studied at Alexandria.

AN ENQUIRY INTO THE DOCTRINES OF
PHILO JUDÆUS.

Num censes igitur subtiliore ratione opus esse ad hæc refellenda ? Nam mentem, fidem, spem, virtutem, honorem, victoriam, salutem, concordiam ceteraque ejusmodi, rerum vim habere videmus, non Deorum.—Cic. de Nat. Deor. III. 24.

BEFORE I enter upon this enquiry, I wish to remark, that it is confined entirely to the opinions of Philo himself. I do not mean to determine any thing about the doctrines of the Jews relative to the divine nature in the time of Philo: though all expositions of them, which are founded upon different interpretations of Philo, must, as far as they depend upon such interpretations, be affected by my reasonings, if they be allowed to be valid. Least of all would I have it supposed, that I mean to deny that many passages of the Old Testament refer to the second person of the ever-blessed Trinity, when I deny that Philo's interpretations of them have any such reference.

A distinguished [1] writer upon this subject has affirmed that Philo was not a Platonist. If he had meant by this assertion that Philo did not adopt all the opinions of Plato, it must have been admitted. For it was scarcely possible for him to do this, without abandoning the religion of his fathers, which, with all his bias towards philo-

[1] Allix's *Judgment of the Jewish Church*, p. 354.

sophy, he does not appear to have entertained any thought of doing. But the author, to whom I refer, goes farther. He says, Philo had been so little acquainted with Plato's works, that he brings some of Plato's opinions upon the credit of Aristotle[2]. It is a question of words, whether he should be called a Platonist or an Eclectic; because he did not abandon Judaism, and, embracing all the opinions, prove his doctrines by the authority of Plato. But it is of importance to the present enquiry to shew, that Philo was so well acquainted with the principles of Plato, that he made great use of them in his own theological works.

Philo has adopted Plato's division of things into the two great classes, Intelligibles and Sensibles (νοητὰ καὶ αἰσθητὰ), the former of which he characterizes in the language of Plato, as always the same in their properties and relations (ἀεὶ κατὰ τὰ αὐτὰ καὶ ὡσαύτως ἔχοντα); but the latter he states, on the contrary, to be subject to perpetual changes (πᾶν γὰρ τὸ αἰσθητὸν ἐν γενέσει καὶ μεταβολαῖς, οὐδέποτε κατὰ τὰ αὐτὰ ὄν.) Like him in *Philebus*, he calls the stars living and intelligent beings (ζῶά τε εἶναι λέγονται καὶ ζῶα νοερά;) where likewise he says, that man derives his ideas of music, and virtue, which consists in well-harmonized affections, from the harmony that is conspicuous in the works of creation. From this men, who were formed after them, inscribed on their

De Opificio Mundi, p. 2.

p. 16.

70

---

[2] I presume he alludes to what Philo says, Περὶ Ἀφθαρσίας Κόσμου, p. 941.

own souls, and delivered down the most necessary and most profitable rules of life (ἀφ' ἧς οἱ μετὰ ταῦτα ἄνθρωποι ἐγγραψάμενοι ταῖς ἑαυτῶν ψυχαῖς ἀναγκαιοτάτην καὶ ὠφελιμωτάτην τέχνην τῷ βίῳ παρέδοσαν. In conformity with this doctrine, he styles wisdom a well-harmonized and completely musical symphony of virtues (εὐάρμοστον καὶ πάμμουσον συμφωνίαν ἀρετῶν.) In the same language he describes vicious folly to be an inharmonious, discordant, untuneful symphony (ἀνάρμοστον καὶ ἐκμελῆ καὶ ἄμουσον συμφωνίαν.) Again, as Plato in his *Timæus* calls time an image of eternity, so Philo calls eternity the archetype and pattern of time (ἀρχέτυπον τοῦ χρόνου καὶ παράδειγμα αἰών).

<small>p. 17.</small>
<small>Περὶ συγχ. διαλεκτ. p. 326.</small>
<small>p. 322.</small>
<small>Περὶ τοῦ ὅτι ἄτρεπτον τὸ θεῖον. p. 298.</small>

But, above all, it is most evident that he had the *Timæus* of Plato in his eye when he wrote his treatise of the Creation of the World, and that he grounded his explanations upon the same principles. Thus, having divided things into intelligible, which are eternal, unchangeable and permanent; and sensible, which are generated, are changeable and fleeting; he enquires, whether the world had a beginning. This question he answers as readily as Plato did, and upon the same principle: Since it is visible and the object of sense, it must have been made (ἐπεὶ οὖν ὁρατός τε καὶ αἰσθητὸς ὅδε ὁ κόσμος, ἀναγκαίως ἂν εἴη καὶ γενητός.) This is precisely the reason which was before assigned by Plato in *Timæus* for the world's having had a beginning: It was made; for it is visible and tangible, and has a body, that is, a body of

<small>[p. 3.]</small>

66   *Doctrines of* PHILO JUDÆUS.

[p. 28 B.] gross matter (γέγονεν· ὁρατὸς γὰρ ἁπτός τέ ἐστι καὶ σῶμα ἔχων).

Again Philo tells us, that God foresaw that an imitation could not be beautiful without a beautiful pattern; and that nothing material was faultless, which had not been framed according to an archetype and intelligible idea. On this account, when he resolved to create this visible world, he first modelled the intelligible one, that by this incorporeal and most divine pattern he might construct the material world[3]. This material world, which was to be the image of the intelligible, was to contain as many kinds of sensible beings as there were intelligibles in the pattern[4]. This intelligible world, according to Philo, was composed of ideas. It is not allowable, he said, to affirm or suppose that it subsisted in any place. But we shall know where it did subsist, by pursuing the analogy of things in ourselves[5]. When a city is to be built for some great prince or potentate, a man, well-instructed in architecture, comes forward, and, having examined the situation, first describes within himself almost all the parts of the

---

[3] Προλαβὼν ὁ Θεὸς ἅτε Θεὸς, ὅτι μίμημα καλὸν οὐκ ἄν ποτε γένοιτο καλοῦ δίχα παραδείγματος, οὐδέ τι τῶν αἰσθητῶν ἀνυπαίτιον, ὃ μὴ πρὸς ἀρχέτυπον καὶ νοητὴν ἰδέαν ἀπεικονίσθη, βουληθεὶς τὸν ὁρατὸν τουτονὶ κόσμον δημιουργῆσαι, προεξετύπου τὸν νοητὸν, ἵνα χρώμενος ἀσωμάτῳ καὶ θεοειδεστάτῳ παραδείγματι, τὸν σωματικὸν ἀπεργάσηται, p. 3. In this passage he clearly had in his eye the following one of Plato upon the same subject in the dialogue above mentioned: Ὅπου μὲν οὖν ἂν ὁ δημιουργὸς, πρὸς τὸ κατὰ ταὐτὰ ἔχον βλέπων ἀεὶ, τοιούτῳ τινὶ προσχρώμενος παραδείγματι τὴν ἰδέαν καὶ δύναμιν ἀπεργάζηται, καλὸν ἐξ ἀνάγκης οὕτως ἀποτελεῖσθαι πᾶν· οὗ δ' ἂν εἰς τὸ γεγονὸς, γεννητῷ παραδείγματι

Doctrines of PHILO JUDÆUS. 67

city that is to be built, temples, places of exercise, courts of justice, market-places, harbours, docks, &c. Then, having received the types of each of them in his mind, as in wax, he frames an intelligible city, and stamps the images of the several parts on his memory. To this model he looks 73 when he begins to execute his well-arranged plan with stone and wood, making the material substances like each of the incorporeal ideas. Something of this kind must we conceive of God, who, having purposed to build a capital city, first imagined the types of it; of which he constituted the intelligible world, and then used it as a pattern, when he finished the sensible world. As therefore the city, predelineated in the architect, had no external place, but was stamped upon the mind of the artist; in the same manner also the world composed of ideas cannot have any other place than the divine intellect, which arranged it.

Having discoursed a little upon the cause of God's creating the world, he returns to his analogy. If, says he, any one would use plain words, unadorned by figures, he would say, that the intel-

προσχρώμενος, οὐ καλόν, p. 28. [B].

4 Πρεσβυτέρου νεώτερον ἀπεικόνισμα, τοσαῦτα περιέξοντα αἰσθητὰ γένη, ὅσαπερ ἐν ἐκείνῳ νοητά, [p. 3.] This is evidently taken from the description which Plato gave of the pattern, according to which the Creator formed the present world: τὰ γὰρ δὴ νοητὰ ζῶα πάντα ἐκεῖνο ἐν ἑαυτῷ περιλαβὸν ἔχει, καθάπερ ὅδε ὁ κόσμος ἡμᾶς, ὅσα τε ἄλλα θρέμματα συνέστηκεν ὁρατά.—[Timæus, p. 30 D.]

5 Τὸν δὲ ἐκ τῶν ἰδεῶν συνεστῶτα κόσμον ἐν τόπῳ τινὶ λέγειν ἢ ὑπονοεῖν, οὐ θεμιτόν· ᾗ δ' ὑφέστηκεν εἰσόμεθα, παρακολουθήσαντες εἰκόνι τινὶ τῶν παρ' ἡμῖν. [p. 4].

D 5

ligible world is nothing else but the [6] intellect of God, while he was now making the world. For the intelligible city is nothing else but the reasoning of the architect, while he is now projecting to build the material city.

The plain meaning of all this is, that the divine Being, when he purposed to create the world, first conceived ideas of the several parts of which it was to consist. These ideas he formed into one plan, and thus constituted the intelligible world. This he used as a pattern in his creation of the material world, which he made to correspond with it in every particular, the several substances which composed the one answering to the several ideas which composed the other. It is not allowable to assert or suppose that this intelligible world, thus composed of ideas, had a real and external existence, as some philosophers may have maintained. It was no more than the ideal plan in the intellect of the Creator; in the same manner as the ideal plan of a city, which is to be built, subsists only in the intellect of the architect, and has no existence external to it. So that, to use plain language, the intelligible world is nothing else but the reasoning of God, when he was about to create the material world; just as the intel-

---

[6] If the reader wishes to see a complete specimen of the exertions of a subtle genius in support of a system, let him look into Norris's *Theory of the Ideal or Intelligible World*. He will there see how much that ingenious writer, aided by St Augustin and Malebranche, could extract from this doctrine.

[7] Τῶν μελλόντων ἀποτελεῖσθαι σωμάτων ἀσωμάτους ἰδέας τῇ ψυχῇ θεωρῶν, πρὸς ἃς ἔδει, καθάπερ ἀπ' ἀρχετύπου γραφῆς καὶ

Doctrines of PHILO JUDÆUS. 69

ligible city was only the reasoning of the architect, when he was about to build a material city. He uses the same language in the third book of the *Life of Moses*, when he is speaking of the pattern of the tabernacle and the several parts of the furniture of it, which was shewed to Moses in the mount, and according to which he formed the earthly tabernacle. The incorporeal ideas, which were impressed upon his mind, served as a pattern according to which he formed the material objects[7].

Philo was not satisfied with giving this general account of the nature of the intelligible world. He proceeded to state the principal parts of which it was composed, and the order in which they were framed. First, the Creator formed in the intelligible world an incorporeal heaven and an invisible earth, and the idea of air, and a void: then the incorporeal essence of water, and breath or spirit, and light, which was also incorporeal, and the intelligible pattern of the sun, and of all the luminous stars, that were to subsist throughout the heaven.

In his treatise Περὶ τοῦ τίς ὁ τῶν θείων πραγμάτων κληρόνομος, he attributes the formation of things to the art of God (ἡ τοῦ Θεοῦ τέχνη— p. 502. δεδημιούργηκε.) And again he styles nature the sacred logos or reason (ἡ φύσις—ὁ ἱερὸς λόγος). p. 506.

νοητῶν παραδειγμάτων αἰσθητὰ μιμήματα ἀπεικονισθῆναι—ὁ μὲν οὖν τύπος τοῦ παραδείγματος ἐνεσφραγίζετο τῇ διανοίᾳ τοῦ προφήτου, διαζωγραφούμενος καὶ προδιαπλαττόμενος ἀφανῶς ἄνευ ὕλης ἀοράτοις εἴδεσι· τὸ δ' ἀποτέλεσμα πρὸς τὸν τύπον ἐδημιουργεῖτο, ἐναποματτομένου τὰς σφραγῖδας τοῦ τεχνίτου ταῖς προσφόροις ἑκάστῳ ὑλικαῖς οὐσίαις. [p. 665.]

If it had been the professed design of Philo to guard against the possibility of annexing a distinct personality to Λόγος θεῖος or Λόγος θεοῦ, which I have rendered 'the divine intellect' and 'the intellect of God,' I do not see how he could have used terms more precise, or illustrations more apposite.

Yet the author, to whom I before referred, has maintained that the passages in Philo for the existence of the Λόγος, as a person coeternal with the Father, are so evident, that they cannot be denied. Indeed he conceives them to be so evident, that, though he has quoted abundantly upon the same subject from the Chaldee Paraphrasts, yet he rests the weight of his cause upon Philo, who, he says, writ much larger and clearer than they did; and will contribute to explain some of the quotations taken out of the *Paraphrases* in use at Babylon and Jerusalem.

However, notwithstanding this confidence in the authority of Philo, and in the propriety of his own interpretations of his doctrines, he makes some concessions, which detract much from the efficacy of either the authority or the interpretation. 'After all that I have alleged from Philo and the *Paraphrases*,' says he, 'I do not pretend to affirm that they had as distinct notions of the Trinity as we have; nor do I deny but that sometimes they put a different construction on the texts which we have cited in proof of this mystery: nay, I own that their ideas are often confused when they speak of these things, and par-

77 ticularly they refer sometimes that to the second person which should be ascribed to the third, and that to the third which properly belongs to the second.'

But this is not all. He allows that Philo, in one instance at least, fell into error by endea- vouring to accommodate Moses his notions to the notions of a particular philosophy. He next admits that Philo, who had gathered his notions, as other Jews did, from reading the books of the Old Testament, together with their traditional interpretations, was not so much a master of them as to make them always consist with one another. In the next sentence he does not deny that Philo was not constant to himself. Indeed he could not deny this; as he had himself before charged him with inconsistency, in making God, when he was engaged in his work of creation, address himself to the angels, and employ them as assistants in his work.

p. 154.

pp. 155, 156.

De Confusion. Ling. p. 349.

pp. 128, 129.

An animated and ingenious [8]writer of the pre-

---

[8] Whitaker, in his *History of Arianism*. Without entering into the general merits of the question discussed by this learned author, I beg leave to make a remark upon his interpretation of a passage of Scripture, which appears to me not to be well founded. St Matthew, xxii. 34, tells us, that when our Saviour had answered the ensnaring question of the Sadducees concerning the resurrection, the Pharisees also assembled, and put a question to him on their part. St Mark, xii. 28, informs us, that the Pharisee who put the question was a scribe. But Mr W. asserts, that these scribes were outwardly Pharisees and inwardly Sadducees, that they came in to the aid of the baffled Sadducees, and that our Saviour alluded to this repugnance between their external profession and internal sentiments, when

sent day, who has trodden boldly in the steps of
Allix, and enforced the same mode of interpretation with great energy, has been obliged, in support of that mode, to impute to Philo not only
p. 36.   exertions of his fancy at the expence of his judg-
p. 107. ment, but also a spirit of subtilizing *being* into *power*, and of dividing the Logos in two.

I readily allow that Philo's interpretations of Scripture are generally very fanciful, and that his works exhibit a curious mixture of Pagan philosophy and Rabbinical learning. But I am persuaded that many of those inconsistencies, and all

> he addressed this question to them, 'What think ye of Christ? Whose son is he?'
> I dissent from this explanation for the following reasons. First, Neither of the Evangelists, who mention the transaction, give any direct intimation that they were inwardly Sadducees. They call them simply either Pharisees or scribes. Secondly, St Mark says, that the scribe who put the question to Jesus knew that he had answered the Sadducees properly (εἰδὼς, ὅτι καλῶς αὐτοῖς ἀπεκρίθη). This he would not have known, or have thought, if he had been a Sadducee. Thirdly, St Mark says, that Jesus, perceiving that the scribe who had asked him the question, replied intelligently (νουνεχῶς), said to him, 'Thou art not far from the kingdom of God.' Fourthly, St Mark says, 'That Christ, as he was teaching publickly in the temple, asked, How say the *scribes*, that Christ is the son of David?' Whereby it seems to be implied, not merely, that it was the opinion of those particular men then present, but that it was the established opinion of the doctors of the Law. Fifthly, the question is put by St Luke, xx. 41, in terms still more general: 'How say *they*, that Christ is David's son?' By this it may be intimated, that it was the received opinion of the Jews in general at that time. Mr Whitaker supposes, that a difference between the opinion of the scribes and that of the people at large is intimated by the evangelist, Mark xii. 37, when he subjoins, 'the common people heard him gladly.' It is surely taking too much for granted to maintain, that our Saviour's reasons would not

Doctrines of PHILO JUDÆUS.

that spirit of subtilizing being into power, with which he has been charged, are not justly to be imputed to him, but to his interpreters, who have not attended to the avowed design of his writings, and to the principles which he laid down for the accomplishment of that design.

The design itself he declares explicitly in his Treatise Περὶ Συγχύσεως Διαλεκτῶν; in which he [p. 819.] undertakes to shew, that under the literal narrative is contained a moral or spiritual meaning, which is to be considered as the true sense, the other being only a shadow[9]. After he had gone through

---

have been able to work conviction in the people, unless they had been 'consentaneous to all their notions of the Messiah,' p. 410. It is fully as natural to suppose, that the common people, not having speculated so much upon the subject, and being less enslaved by preconceived opinions and rooted prejudices, were more open to conviction, and more ready to acknowledge the justness of his reasonings. St Mark, vi. 20, uses the same expression, when he speaks of the manner in which Herod heard John the Baptist; in which passage it is scarcely to be conceived that he has any allusion to Herod's preconceived opinions. Again, in the *Acts of the Apostles*, xvii. 11, it is said, 'That the Bereans received the word with all readiness of mind,' (μετὰ πάσης προθυμίας). Yet this word, which they thus received, appears to have been so far from being consentaneous to all their previous notions of the Messiah, that they searched the Scriptures daily, to see whether those things were so. Sixthly, These men must have been very shallow pretenders indeed, if, when a question of that kind was asked them in public by a person, whom they had obviously been endeavouring to ensnare, they should immediately return an answer according to their concealed opinions and not according to their outward profession. Without, therefore, forming a precise opinion of the system maintained by the learned author, I think he can derive no support for it from the transaction in question.

[9] Origen adopted from Philo the principal of allegorizing the Scriptures. His account of it is thus rendered by his transla-

the whole of his explanation, These, says he, are my opinions. Others, following the plain and obvious meaning of the words, think that the origin of the Greek and Barbarian languages is here described. I do not censure them. Perhaps they also give a true account. I would, however, exhort them not to rest in it, but to pass on to the figurative interpretations, and assure themselves that the literal circumstances recorded in the Scriptures are, as it were, shadows of bodies, but that the qualities indicated by them are the things which in reality subsist[10].

It is natural to suppose, that a man who deals in such subtilties should occasionally vary in the degrees of his refinements. He may also naturally be expected to be sometimes led into a seeming inaccuracy of expression, by his having in some respects adopted the sentiments and in more respects the expressions of Plato. But it is not so natural to suppose that he should argue upon contradictory principles, which are generally the result of cooler judgment and more deliberate consideration. Nor is it quite so customary for a writer to subtilize being into power, as it is to personify power, and by so doing to invest it with a figurative being.

But whatever judgment may be formed of these

tor: *Cum ergo de his talibus et horum similibus Spiritui Sancto esset intentio illuminare sanctas animas, quæ se mysterio dederant veritatis; secundo loco habetur ille prospectus, ut propter eos, qui vel non possent vel nollent huic se labori atque industriæ tradere, quo hæc tanta et talia doceri vel agnoscere mererentur, involveret et occultaret sermonibus usitatis sub prætextu historiæ cujusdam et narrationis rerum visibilium arcana mysteria.* — Περὶ Ἀρχῶν. Lib. IV. cap. 11.

observations, every body, I think, must allow, that Philo himself is the best explainer of his own principles; and that those, which he has exhibited in his cooler moments, must be the genuine interpretations of them, how extravagantly soever he may seem to have refined upon them in the fervor of his imagination.

I have already shewn how careful he was to inculcate upon his readers, in the beginning of his treatise Περὶ Κοσμοποιίας, that κόσμος νοητός, which he placed in the intellect of the Deity, and which he sometimes denominated the divine intellect, meant nothing more than the abstract design or the reason of God, when he purposed to create the world; and was similar to the plan of a city formed in the mind of an architect. Most of the authors who have written upon this subject, instead of taking this declaration as a guide, when they examine what Mr Whitaker calls the exertions of his fancy at the expence of his judgment, have collected a multitude of detached passages seemingly attributing a direct personality and agency to the λόγος, and have applied the conclusions, deduced from them, to what they call an explanation of this clear and explicit declaration. I shall therefore take the several appellations by which the Logos has been

10 [Ταῦτα μὲν ἡμεῖς· οἱ δὲ τοῖς ἐμφανέσι καὶ προχείροις μόνον ἐπακολουθοῦντες οἴονται γένεσιν διαλεκτῶν Ἑλλήνων τε καὶ Βαρβάρων ὑπογράφεσθαι—οὓς οὐκ ἂν αἰτιασάμενος—ἴσως γὰρ ἀληθεῖ καὶ αὐτοὶ χρῶνται λόγῳ—παρακελεύσαιμ' ἂν, μὴ ἐπὶ τούτων στῆναι, μετελθεῖν δὲ ἐπὶ τὰς τροπικὰς ἀποδόσεις, νομίσαντας τὰ μὲν ῥητὰ τῶν χρησμῶν σκιάς τινας ὡσανεὶ σωμάτων εἶναι, τὰς δ' ἐμφαινομένας δυνάμεις τὰ ὑφεστῶτα ἀληθείᾳ πράγματα.]

denominated, and consider a few instances under each, which may serve to explain all others of the same class.

First, we will consider it as being the image of God (εἰκών) and the shadow of God (σκία). Philo has explicitly declared, in the explanation of Beseleel, how κόσμος νοητός, the *intelligible world*, the reason or intellect of God, the abstract form of the universe, is entitled to these appellations. "The shadow of God is his λόγος, or reason, which he used as an instrument or organ, when he made the world. This shadow and image is also another archetype. For as God is the pattern of the image which we have now called the shadow; in the same manner the image is the pattern of other things[11]."

[*Legis Allegor.* III. § 31, p. 79.]

Having thus shewn that the pattern and shadow and image are relative terms, and that κόσμος νοητός, the intelligible world, which he also calls λόγος θεοῦ, and which is the pattern of the sensible world, is also itself the shadow or image of God, he proceeds to shew in what sense it is the shadow. "The wisest philosophers have maintained, that it

[§ 32, p. 79.]

---

[11] [Σκιὰ θεοῦ δὲ ὁ λόγος αὐτοῦ ἐστιν, ᾧ καθάπερ ὀργάνῳ προσχρησάμενος ἐκοσμοποίει. Αὕτη δὲ ἡ σκιὰ καὶ τὸ ὡσανεὶ ἀπεικόνισμα ἑτέρων ἐστὶν ἀρχέτυπον. Ὥσπερ γὰρ ὁ θεὸς παράδειγμα τῆς εἰκόνος, ἣν σκιὰν νυνὶ κέκληκεν, οὕτως ἡ εἰκὼν ἄλλων γίγνεται παράδειγμα.]

[12] [Οἱ δοκοῦντες ἄριστα φιλοσοφεῖν ἔφασαν, ὅτι ἀπὸ τοῦ κόσμου καὶ τῶν μερῶν αὐτοῦ καὶ τῶν ἐνυπαρχουσῶν τούτοις δυνάμεων ἀντίληψιν ἐποιησάμεθα τοῦ αἰτίου. Ὥσπερ γὰρ εἴ τις ἴδοι δεδημιουργημένην οἰκίαν ἐπιμελῶς, προπυλαίοις, στοαῖς, ἀνδρῶσι, γυναικωνίτισι, τοῖς ἄλλοις οἰκοδομήμασιν, ἔννοιαν λήψεται τοῦ τεχνίτου,—οὐ γὰρ ἄνευ τέχνης καὶ δημιουργοῦ νομιεῖ τὴν οἰκίαν ἀποτελεσθῆναι, τὸν αὐτὸν δὲ τρόπον καὶ ἐπὶ πόλεως, καὶ νεὼς, καὶ παντὸς ἐλάττονος ἢ

is from the world and its parts and their powers that we must derive our conception of its author. For if a person should see a house, a city, a temple, or any other building, constructed with their several parts harmonizing with each other, he would form a conception of an artist. For he would suppose that those things could not have been executed without skill and a builder. So also, when a person has entered into this world, as into a very great house or city, and has beheld the heaven revolving in a circle, and all things contained within it; and the planets and fixed stars moving harmoniously, &c.—and moreover, living beings, mortal and immortal, and different kinds of plants and fruits; he will truly reason, that those things were not formed without perfect art; but that God was and is the disposer of this universe. They, who reason thus, have a conception of God by means of his shadow, forming a notion of the artist by means of his works[12].

84 The plain meaning of this is, that the mind of man in its natural state, represented by Beseleel, is not able by its own strength to attain any idea

μείζονος κατασκευάσματος—οὕτω δὴ καὶ εἰσελθών τις ὥσπερ εἰς μεγίστην οἰκίαν ἢ πόλιν τόνδε τὸν κόσμον, καὶ θεασάμενος οὐρανὸν ἐν κύκλῳ περιπολοῦντα, καὶ πάντα ἐντὸς συνειληφότα, πλανήτας δὲ καὶ ἀπλανεῖς ἀστέρας κατὰ ταὐτὰ καὶ ὡσαύτως κινουμένους, ἐμμελῶς τε καὶ ἐναρμονίως, καὶ τῷ παντὶ ὠφελίμως, γῆν δὲ τὸν μεσαίτατον χῶρον λαχοῦσαν, ὕδατός τε καὶ ἀέρος χύσεις ἐν μεθορίῳ τεταγμένας, ἔτι δὲ ζῶα θνητά τε αὖ καὶ ἀθάνατα, καὶ φυτῶν καὶ καρπῶν διαφορὰς, λογιεῖται δήπου, ὅτι ταῦτα οὐκ ἄνευ τέχνης παντελοῦς δεδημιούργηται, ἀλλὰ καὶ ἦν καὶ ἔστιν ὁ τοῦδε τοῦ παντὸς δημιουργὸς ὁ θεός. Οἱ δὴ οὕτως ἐπιλογιζόμενοι, διὰ σκιᾶς τὸν θεὸν καταλαμβάνουσι, διὰ τῶν ἔργων τὸν τεχνίτην κατανοοῦντες.]

of the Deity, but by contemplating those marks of his attributes which he has impressed upon his works. These exhibit an image and reflect a shadow of the Supreme self-existent Being. But the perfect and thoroughly-purified mind, represented by Moses, which is initiated into the great mysteries, does not acquire its knowledge of the author from the things that were made, of the permanent being from the shadow; but, rising above what was made, receives a manifest representation of him, so as to derive from himself a conception of him and his shadow, which was, his Logos and this world[13].

This process of the understanding in tracing out the Deity through the sensible and intelligible world is described in a similar manner in his Treatise Περὶ Κοσμοποιίας. "The mind, having traversed sea and land, and surveyed the several natures, rises into the air, and examines its several productions; whence it is carried higher into the ether and the heavenly courses of the stars. Thence, led by a love of wisdom, it is elevated

---

[13] ["Εστι δέ τις τελεώτερος καὶ μᾶλλον κεκαθαρμένος νοῦς, τὰ μεγάλα μυστήρια μυηθείς, ὅστις οὐκ ἀπὸ τῶν γεγονότων τὸ αἴτιον γνωρίζει, ὡς ἂν ἀπὸ σκιᾶς τὸ μένον· ἀλλ' ὑπερκύψας τὸ γεννητὸν, ἔμφασιν ἐναργῆ τοῦ ἀγεννήτου λαμβάνει, ὡς ἀπ' αὐτοῦ αὐτὸν καταλαμβάνειν, καὶ τὴν σκιὰν αὐτοῦ, ὅπερ ἦν, τόν τε λόγον καὶ τόνδε τὸν κόσμον.]

[14] [Καὶ τέχναις καὶ ἐπιστήμαις πολυσχιδεῖς τε ἀνατέμνων ὁδοὺς, καὶ λεωφόρους ἀπάσας, διὰ γῆς ἔρχεται καὶ θαλάττης, τὰ ἐν ἑκατέρα φύσει διερευνώμενος. Καὶ πάλιν πτηνὸς ἀρθεὶς, καὶ τὸν ἀέρα καὶ τὰ τούτου παθήματα κατασκεψάμενος, ἀνωτέρω φέρεται πρὸς αἰθέρα καὶ τὰς οὐρανίους περιόδους. Πλανήτων τε καὶ ἀπλανῶν χορείαις συμπεριπολυθεὶς κατὰ τοὺς τῆς μουσικῆς τελείους νόμους, ἑπόμενος ἔρωτι σοφίας ποδηγετοῦντι, πᾶσαν τὴν αἰσθητὴν οὐσίαν ὑπερκύψας, ἐν-

Doctrines of PHILO JUDÆUS. 79

above all sensible, and advances to the intelligible essence; and, having contemplated in it the patterns and ideas of those sensible things which it saw here, surpassing beauty, it is seized with a sober ebriety, and grows frantic like the Corybantes, being filled with a different and better desire and longing, by which it is conducted to the very highest top of the intelligibles, and seems to proceed to the great king himself. But while it desires to see him, the pure and unmixed splendors of heavenly light rush forth as a torrent, so as to darken the eye of the understanding with their brightness [14]."

Moreover, the Deity is said to be attended by two shadows, which are also called [15] powers (δυνάμεις), *De Abrahamo*, p. 367. By means of these there is a threefold representation of one subject. Not that, properly speaking, there can be any shadows of God; but the term is used in a figurative sense to assist the illustration of the subject. In the middle is the Father of all, who is called in the Holy Scriptures the existent Being, and on each hand are the oldest and nearest powers of the

ταῦθα ἐφίεται τῆς νοητῆς. καὶ ὧν εἶδεν ἐνταῦθα αἰσθητῶν, ἐν ἐκείνῃ τὰ παραδείγματα καὶ τὰς ἰδέας θεασάμενος, ὑπερβάλλοντα κάλλη, μέθῃ νηφαλίῳ κατασχεθεὶς, ὥσπερ οἱ κορυβαντιῶντες, ἐνθουσιᾷ, ἑτέρου γεμισθεὶς ἱμέρου καὶ πόθου βελτίονος, ὑφ' οὗ πρὸς τὴν ἄκραν ἀψῖδα παραπεμφθεὶς τῶν νοητῶν ἐπ' αὐτὸν ἰέναι δοκεῖ τὸν μέγαν βασιλέα. Γλιχομένου δὲ ἰδεῖν, θείου φωτὸς ἄκρατοι καὶ ἀμιγεῖς αὐγαὶ χειμάρρου τρόπον ἐκχέονται, ὡς ταῖς μαρμαρυγαῖς τὸ τῆς διανοίας ὄμμα σκοτοδινιᾶν.]

[15] Plato in his Dialogue *De Rep.* Lib. v. p. 477. [c], gives this definition of powers: Φήσομεν δυνάμεις εἶναι γένος τι ὄντων, αἷς δὴ καὶ ἡμεῖς δυνάμεθα ἃ δυνάμεθα—and knowledge he denominates the most energetic of all powers: Πασῶν γε δυνάμεων ἐρρωμενεστάτην.

existent Being, which are denominated the creative and the regal powers. The creative power is God; for by this he founded and arranged the world. 86 The regal power is Lord; for that which made has a just right to control and govern what is made. Thus, being in the middle, and attended by each of his powers, he presents an appearance sometimes of one, sometimes of three : of one, to the completely purified mind that can attain to the simple and complete idea without any other aid; of three, to the mind that cannot form a conception of existence from itself alone without something else, but conceives of it from its actions either as creating or as governing[16].

When the supreme Being is called the existent, he is spoken of in an absolute sense, and by his proper denomination (κυρίως); but when he is called God, it is catachrestically: for those several powers, which he exerted in the creation, express not the

[16] [Μὴ μέντοι νομισάτω τις ἐπὶ θεοῦ τὰς σκιὰς κυριολογεῖσθαι· κατάχρησις ὀνόματος αὐτὸ μόνον ἐστὶ, πρὸς ἐναργεστέραν ἔμφασιν τοῦ δηλουμένου πράγματος. Ἐπεὶ τό γε ἀληθὲς οὐχ οὕτως ἔχει· ἀλλ' ἔστιν, ὡς ἄν τις τῆς ἀληθείας ἐγγύτατα ἱστάμενος εἴποι, πατὴρ μὲν τῶν ὅλων ὁ μέσος, ὃς ἐν ταῖς ἱεραῖς γραφαῖς κυρίῳ ὀνόματι καλεῖται ὁ Ὤν· αἱ δὲ παρ' ἑκάτερα πρεσβύταται καὶ ἐγγύταται τοῦ ὄντος δυνάμεις, ὧν ἡ μὲν ποιητική, ἡ δὲ αὖ βασιλικὴ προσαγορεύεται. Καὶ ἡ μὲν ποιητικὴ Θεός· ταύτῃ γὰρ ἔθηκέ τε καὶ διεκόσμησε τὸ πᾶν. Ἡ δὲ βασιλικὴ κύριος· θέμις γὰρ ἄρχειν καὶ κρατεῖν τὸ πεποιηκὸς τοῦ γενομένου. Δορυφορούμενος οὖν ὁ μέσος ὑφ' ἑκατέρας τῶν δυνάμεων παρέχει τῇ ὁρατικῇ διανοίᾳ τοτὲ μὲν ἑνὸς, τοτὲ δὲ τριῶν φαντασίαν· ἑνὸς μὲν, ὅταν ἄκρως καθαρθεῖσα ἡ ψυχὴ, καὶ μὴ μόνον τὰ πλήθη τῶν ἀριθμῶν, ἀλλὰ καὶ τὴν γείτονα μονάδος δυάδα ὑπερβᾶσα, πρὸς τὴν ἀμιγῆ καὶ ἀσύμπλοκον καὶ καθ' αὑτὴν οὐδενὸς ἐπιδεᾶ τὸ παράπαν ἰδέαν ἐπείγηται· τριῶν δὲ, ὅταν μήπω τὰς μεγάλας τελεσθεῖσα τελετὰς, ἔτι ἐν ταῖς βραχυτέραις ὀργιάζηται, καὶ μὴ

principle of his existence, but his relations to other things (ὡσανεὶ πρὸς τί). As, when his regal and beneficent powers are spoken of, he must be a king of some thing, and a benefactor of some thing; that which is governed or benefited being altogether distinct from it. Akin to these is also his creative power, which is called God: for by this power, the father, who begat and framed, established all things. Περὶ τῶν Μετονομαζομένων, p. 1048.[17]

It may be proper to observe, that in the former instances which I quoted, the image, or shadow of God, is spoken of as one, as it referred to that power of God which was delineated and shadowed out in the creation of the world; but in the latter quotations, there is also another shadow of him, as governor and judge of that world which he created. Those who have maintained from this and other similar passages, that Philo had a knowledge of a plurality of persons in the Godhead, have done it principally to shew, that he had a more accurate

δύνηται τὸ ὂν ἄνευ ἑτέρου τινὸς ἐξ αὐτοῦ μόνου καταλαβεῖν, ἀλλὰ διὰ τῶν δρωμένων, ἢ κτίζον ἢ ἄρχον.]

[17] [Ἀλλὰ γὰρ οὐδ' ἐκεῖνο προσῆκεν ἀγνοεῖν, ὅτι τὸ ἐγώ εἰμι θεὸς σὸς λέγεται καταχρηστικῶς οὐ κυρίως. Τὸ γὰρ ὄν, ᾗ ὄν ἐστιν, οὐχὶ τῶν πρός τι· αὐτὸ γὰρ ἑαυτοῦ πλῆρες, καὶ αὐτὸ ἑαυτῷ ἱκανὸν, καὶ πρὸ τῆς τοῦ κόσμου γενέσεως, καὶ μετὰ τὴν γένεσιν τοῦ παντὸς ἐν ὁμοίῳ. Ἄτρεπτον γὰρ καὶ ἀμετάβλητον, χρῇζον ἑτέρου τὸ παράπαν οὐδενὸς, ὥστε αὐτοῦ μὲν εἶναι τὰ πάντα, μηδενὸς δὲ κυρίως αὐτό. Τῶν δὲ δυνάμεων, ἃς ἔτεινεν εἰς γένεσιν ἐπ' εὐεργεσίᾳ τοῦ συσταθέντος, ἐνίας συμβέβηκε λέγεσθαι ὡσανεὶ πρός τι, τὴν βασιλικὴν, τὴν εὐεργετικήν· βασιλεὺς γάρ τινος καὶ εὐεργέτης τινὸς, ἑτέρου πάντως βασιλευομένου καὶ εὐεργετουμένου. Τούτων συγγενής ἐστι καὶ ἡ ποιητικὴ δύναμις, ἡ καλουμένη θεός· διὰ γὰρ ταύτης τῆς δυνάμεως ἔθηκε τὰ πάντα ὁ γεννήσας καὶ τεχνιτεύσας πατήρ, ὥστε τὸ "ἐγώ εἰμι θεὸς σὸς" ἴσον ἐστὶ τῷ "ἐγώ εἰμι ποιητὴς καὶ δημιουργός."]

knowledge of the divine nature than he could be supposed to have had, if he had conceived it to have been in all respects a simple monad, as much one in personality as in essence. Whereas Philo says, that the terms are catachrestically used which represent him under the appearance of three, as the existent[18] Being attended on either hand by those two of his powers which were first exerted, and are most closely and intimately connected with his essence, viz. first, his power of creation, and secondly, his power of governing that which he had created.

This mode of expression and illustration was adopted, he said, in order to aid the conceptions of imperfect minds, which are unable to comprehend the simplicity of one self-existent, independent being, and by arguing *a priori* to perceive how from this pure essence as from their proper fountain, proceed the powers of creation and government, and the several objects upon which those powers are to be employed. Finite intelligences, which cannot thus contemplate him at once in his essence, are obliged as it were to divide him, and view him in detached parts in his acts, but chiefly

---

[18] Origen in his first *Homily* on Isaiah, viz. on chapter vi., seems to have derived his ideas from hence, when he is explaining the vision of the Lord sitting upon a throne high and lifted up, surrounded by Seraphim. The passage is thus rendered by his translator: Si video eum regnantem cœlestibus virtutibus, video eum sedentem super thronum excelsum et elevatum. Quid est, quod dicit, Cœlestibus virtutibus? Throni, dominationes, principatus, potestates, virtutes cœlestes sunt.— Quæ sunt ista duo Seraphim? Dominus meus Jesus et Spiritus Sanctus. Testimonium enim dat Scriptura, quia ejus mundan-

in those acts of his which are prior in time to all others, most immediately arise out of his essence, and extend to all created beings, viz. his acts of creation and government. Thus arguing *a posteriori* they ascend to the summit of intelligibles, and there contemplate images of the power and goodness of the first cause impressed upon his works, and catch as it were a shadow of him who cannot be contemplated in his essence.

These powers are called (Περὶ Χερουβὶμ, p. 112) his goodness and authority or sovereign power, and are denominated the two highest and first powers belonging to the one truly existing God. By his goodness he created the universe, and by his sovereign authority he governs what he created. Between both these is his λόγος, which is expressed by the symbol of the flaming sword. This connects them together; for it is by his λόγος that God is governor and good. This preceded all things, and was meditated before all things, and is conspicuous in all things[19]. Here λόγος is the plan, the design, by which (to speak after the manner of men) God acted in the creation and government of the world. The unity of design in both so connects his goodness and authority, that there are

tur labia ab uno ex seraphim, qui missus est ad auferenda ejus peccata. Unus autem ex seraphim Dominus meus Jesus Christus est, qui ad auferenda peccata nostra a patre missus est.

[19] [p. 113. "Ελεγε δέ μοι, κατὰ τὸν ἕνα ὄντως ὄντα θεὸν δύο τὰς ἀνωτάτω εἶναι καὶ πρώτας δυνάμεις, ἀγαθότητα καὶ ἐξουσίαν. Καὶ ἀγαθότητι μὲν τὸ πᾶν γεγεννηκέναι, ἐξουσίᾳ δὲ τοῦ γεννηθέντος ἄρχειν. Τρίτον δὲ συναγωγὸν ἀμφοῖν μέσον εἶναι λόγον· λόγῳ γὰρ καὶ ἄρχοντα καὶ ἀγαθὸν εἶναι τὸν θεόν. αὐτὸ πάντα φθάσαν παρημείψατο, καὶ πρὸ πάντων νοούμενον καὶ ἐπὶ πᾶσι φαινόμενον].

manifest indications of each in the acts of the other.

When the general design of the universe, formed by the existent Being, is spoken of, it is called λόγος. His several designs of the separate parts, though included in the general design, are called plurally λόγοι, and are said to be sent, as well as the singular: τοὺς ἑαυτοῦ λόγους ἐπικουρίας ἕνεκα τῶν φιλαρέτων ἀποστέλλει. By these powers was formed the incorporeal and intelligible world, the archetype of this which appears, being composed of invisible ideas, as this is of visible bodies.

The supreme Being is perpetually said to be surrounded by these powers, as guards of state and attending ministers, δορυφορουμένῳ πρὸς τῶν δυνάμεων.

Not to mention that Isocrates uses the same expression to signify a person's being guarded by the good-will of the citizens (τῇ τῶν πολιτῶν εὐνοίᾳ δορυφορούμενος); Philo uses it to express the human mind's being attended by the senses, whose business it is to furnish it with notices of colours, sounds, tastes, and smells. Again, wealth, glory, and honours, are said to be the attendant ministers (δορυφόροι) of the body, the senses those of the soul. Again, reasons are said to be the attendants and guards of the soul of the wise: δορυφόροι καὶ ὑπέρμαχοι ψυχῆς. And sacred and holy reasonings and words are called the garrison and sentinels of the soul: ἱεροὺς καὶ ὁσίους λόγους αὐτῆς φρουροὺς καὶ φύλακας ὄντας.

These powers of the one existent Being, and

the external expressions of them, his words and [p. 324.] actions, are said to be spoken of in the Scriptures under the emblems of angels. Thus, when young and old in Sodom are stated to have combined against the angels, the spiritual doctrine contained under that narrative is that there was a general disposition to wickedness; and that young and old, with one accord, as if they had bound themselves together by an oath, set themselves in opposition to the divine words and actions, which it is customary to call angels: Πᾶς δ', ὥς φησιν, ὁ λαὸς περιεκύκλωσαν ἅμα τὴν οἰκίαν, νέοι τε καὶ πρεσβῦται, κατὰ τῶν θείων ἔργων καὶ λόγων συνομοσάμενοι, οὓς καλεῖν ἔθος ἀγγέλους. Again, ἀθανάτοις λόγοις, οὓς καλεῖν ἔθος ἀγγέλους. [Περὶ τοῦ θεοπέμπτ. p. 583.]

One of the passages produced to prove the personality of the λόγος, according to Philo, is that wherein he says that the angel who met Hagar, when she fled from the face of Sarah, and brought [Περὶ Χερουβ. p. 108.] her back, was the divine λόγος. But who or what, according to the same interpretation, was Hagar, and Sarah from whom she fled? By Hagar is meant human discipline and the circle of the arts and sciences, who departed from her mistress, Sarah, the emblem of virtue, and was brought back by the angel, who is the divine λόγος [20] (ὅς ἐστι θεῖος λόγος), which he elsewhere calls [21] right reason

[20] Τὴν μέσην παιδείαν τὴν τοῖς ἐγκυκλίοις χορεύουσαν ὁρῶμεν Ἄγαρ, δὶς μὲν ἐξιοῦσαν ἀπὸ τῆς ἀρχούσης ἀρετῆς Σάρρας, [ἅπαξ δὲ τὴν προτεράν ὁδὸν ὑποστρέφουσαν. ἣ τότε μὲν ἀποδρᾶσα] κατάγεται, ὑπαντήσαντος ἀγγέλου, ὅς ἐστι θεῖος λόγος.
[21] Προστησάμενος τὸν ὀρθὸν αὐτοῦ λόγον, πρωτόγονον υἱόν.

(ὀρθὸς λόγος). Hagar fled to avoid the austere and gloomy life of the virtuous[22]. Afterwards Hagar and her son Ishmael, who signifies the sophist, were driven out by Abraham, an emblem of the wise man, at the instigation of Sarah, perfect virtue or wisdom.

In like manner Philo says (p. 114) that the angel, who stood armed to oppose Balaam, was the λόγος of God. But in order to understand the true meaning of the assertion, it is requisite to consider who or what Balaam was, who is said to have been thus opposed. Balaam, says Philo, signifies a foolish people (μάταιον λαόν) who ride in pursuit of gain upon an ass, which signifies husbandry, merchandize, or any other lucrative employment. When he finds that these stop in their course, and do not carry him to the object at which he aims, he wishes for a sword, that is, a power of reasons and words, to chastise them for the failure. But those things, though destitute of the organs of speech, utter a language more distinct than that of any tongue, and point out to him an angel, that is, the word of God, standing armed with divine vengeance to oppose his progress.

It is manifest that, in these instances, θεῖος λόγος and Θεοῦ λόγος, are no more persons, because

Περὶ Γεωργίας Νῶε, p. 195. Οἶς ἂν ὁ ὀρθὸς λόγος ὑποβάλλῃ πεισθησόμενον, τ. ε. λογισμὸν, ὥσπερ τινὰ δικαστὴν ἀδωροδόκητον. Περὶ τοῦ ὅτι ἄτρεπτ. p. 301. Ὁ θεῖος λόγος—ὁ ὀρθὸς λόγος. Περὶ τοῦ Θεοπέμπτ. p. 583. Ὁ τῆς φύσεως ὀρθὸς λόγος, ὃς κυριωτέρᾳ κλήσει προσονομάζεται, θεσμὸς, νόμος θεῖος ὢν, καθ' ὃν [τὰ προσήκοντα καὶ ἐπιβάλλοντα ἑκάστοις ἀπενεμήθη.] Περὶ Κοσμοπ. p. 33.

Doctrines of PHILO JUDÆUS. 87

they are represented by the emblems of angels, than merchandise or agriculture is an animal, because they are supposed to be represented by the ass. In the same spirit of emblematizing he says, that by [23]Eve is meant the senses. It would be too tedious to discuss the several moral and religious doctrines, supposed to be conveyed under the characters of Cain, Jacob, Laban, his daughters, his cattle, &c. p. 119 : the ark and the animals contained in it, p. 186 : Joseph, his wife, and father-in-law, p. 577 : Rebecca, p. 379 : Leah, and in short all the persons and places mentioned in the Pentateuch. The specimens already given are sufficient to shew that they are emblematic and figurative. Now it is well known that the personality of an emblem by no means proves the personality of the thing signified by that emblem, which is some quality, virtue, or duty, as the general result of the whole story is some moral or religious doctrine, which is inculcated under the form of a narrative.

In the same figurative language the Lord's host signifies the several virtues [24]; and the leader of the Lord's host, that divine order and harmony displayed in the arrangement of the universe, from which men derive the principles of virtue and

---

[22] Ἄγαρ, ἡ μέση καὶ ἐγκύκλιος παιδεία, κἂν τὸν αὐστηρὸν καὶ σκυθρωπὸν τῶν φιλαρέτων ἀποδρᾶναι βίον σπουδάσῃ. p. 109.

[23] Προσηγορικῶς μὲν γυναῖκα, ὀνομαστικῶς δὲ Εὔαν, αἰνιττόμενος αἴσθησιν. Περὶ Χερουβίμ, p. 118.

[24] Στρατὸς δὲ θεῖος αἱ ἀρεταί, φιλοθέων ὑπέρμαχοι ψυχῶν. p. 198.

88   *Doctrines of* PHILO JUDÆUS.

wisdom. It is also called the first-born λόγος, the eldest angel, being as it were the archangel with many names. The sensible world is called the younger son of God, and the intelligible world is called the elder son. In the passage, "The horse and the rider hath he thrown into the sea," the rider, he says, is the mind, and the horse the passions[25]. And when the lawgiver forbids the use of horses in war, he says, he does not speak of real cavalry, which is necessary for both offence and defence, but of the irrational and unrestrained and ungovernable motions of the soul[26]. Virtue in general is expressed by paradise, and the several virtues by the trees planted in it.

The divine λόγος is said to be the cement, the bond of union, by which the several parts of the universe are kept together[27]. But the same properties are likewise ascribed to the order and plan according to which the universe was constructed[28].

Mosheim supposes that Philo (*De Abrahamo,* p. 367) alludes to some among the Jews who asserted the doctrines of three natures in God. Whereas in the passage alluded to Philo appears most evidently to me to be speaking ·of those who are not, as he figuratively expresses it, initiated into the great mysteries, and who are not

---

[25] Τετράπουν καὶ σκιρτητικὸν καὶ ὑπέραυχον—παθῶν τε καὶ κακιῶν ἀλκιμώτατον στῖφος—πρὸς δὲ καὶ ὁ ἐπιβάτης αὐτῶν νοῦς, p. 199.

[26] Ἀλλὰ περὶ τῆς κατὰ ψυχὴν ἀλόγου καὶ ἀμέτρου καὶ ἀπειθοῦς φορᾶς, p. 200.

able to contemplate the existent Being in his simple state, without something else to aid their conceptions. They are therefore obliged to have recourse to his acts, and to consider him as creating or governing, when they endeavour to form a notion of him. Indeed the notion, which is formed in this circuitous manner, partakes of a pious opinion; but that which results from a direct view, does not partake of, but is, a pious opinion, or rather, surpasses opinion and is the truth itself. This is the language in which he generally speaks of the popular and the sublime theology, as distinct from each other in degree rather than in kind.

27 Λόγῳ σφίγγεται θείῳ· κόλλα γάρ ἐστι καὶ δεσμὸς οὗτος, p. 507.
28 Παγκάλῳ τῷ τῆς ἀκολουθίας εἱρμῷ κέχρηται, p. 14. Τάξις δ' ἀκολουθία καὶ εἱρμός ἐστι προηγουμένων τινων και ἑπομένων.

THE FATHERS of the CHRISTIAN CHURCH.

Ἐγέννησε τοίνυν αὐτὸν οὐχ οὕτως, ὡς ἄν τις νοήσειεν ἀνθρώπων, ἀλλ' ὡς οἶδεν αὐτὸς μόνος. οὐ γὰρ τὸ, πῶς ἐγέννησεν, εἰπεῖν ἐπαγγελλόμεθα, ἀλλὰ τὸ, οὐχ οὕτως διαβεβαιούμεθα· καὶ οὐχ ἡμεῖς ἀγνοοῦμεν μόνον τὴν ἐκ πατρὸς τοῦ υἱοῦ γέννησὶν, ἀλλὰ καὶ πᾶσα γεννητὴ φύσις.—Cyril. *Catech.* XI. p. 96.

PHOTIUS informs us that from Philo was derived the allegorical method of interpreting Scripture, which prevailed in the primitive Church. This arose from very natural causes.

First, they who have been favoured with a divine revelation, and have by grace availed themselves of it, enjoy a great and manifest advantage over those who are left in a great measure to the exertions of their own minds, and are obliged to trace out the invisible things of God by intricate reasonings and deductions from the things, which do appear in the constitution and government of the world. What even learned men among the latter do hardly guess and with labour find out, is plain and obvious to the meanest and most uncultivated understandings among the former.

Yet this advantage, great as it really is, has not always been sufficient to satisfy the pretensions of those who have been blessed with a divine revelation. Not contented with the bright sunshine which blazes around them, they will scarcely allow the benighted heathen the dim taper of human reason to guide their steps in their laborious travels over the dark mountains. Whatever the Apostle Paul may have said in his various expostulations with the Gentiles, and particularly in his Epistle to the Romans, there are some far wiser, in their own conceit, than seven men that can render a reason, who boldly maintain, that whatever glimmerings of light the Pagans of old have been able to strike out by mere dint of labour and study, have been all either directly or circuitously derived from the sacred writings[1].

Traces of this opinion are to be found in some degree in the works of ancient authors, both Jewish and Christian, though it did not shoot up to the extravagant height to which some have carried it in later days. I should depart from the tenor of my subject, if I did more than barely mention the well-known example of Josephus among the former. Among the latter, the instances are numerous. As I proceed with my work, I shall, in confirmation of what I have here advanced, produce some strong and pointed passages from Justin Martyr and Clemens Alexandrinus, both of them writers of the second century.

To Christians who had embraced these sentiments, the writings of Philo must have been an invaluable treasure. The manner in which he has applied the principles of Plato to illustrate the Mosaical account of the Creation and other parts of

[1] Ἐξ οὗ (Φίλωνος) οἶμαι καὶ πᾶς ὁ ἀλληγορικὸς τῆς γραφῆς ἐν τῇ ἐκκλησίᾳ λόγος ἔσχεν ἀρχὴν εἰσρυῆναι. Photius, p. 96.

the Old Testament, was admirably calculated to flatter their prejudices, and furnished them with specious arguments in support of the opinion which they so strenuously maintained.

Secondly, many were converted to the Christian religion who had previously made considerable progress in the Platonic or[2] Eclectic Philosophy, and retained many of their former prejudices. Others were struck with the great respect that was paid to philosophy, and with the superior skill which its professors displayed in the arts of controversy. On this account they frequented the schools of Alexandria, in which masters of profound learning and great celebrity explained and inculcated, with bewitching eloquence, the speculations of the sages of ancient Greece.

These men, having the sacred volumes in one hand and the writings of Plato in the other, if they believed them both to be true, must have thought the principles and doctrines of each consistent with those of the other: for it is impossible that one truth should be opposite to, or at variance with, another. To these men, therefore, the writings of Philo must have been as acceptable as to those

[2] The following is a description which Clemens Alexandrinus gives of the Eclectic philosophy. "By philosophy I mean neither the Stoic, nor the Platonic, nor the Epicurean and Aristotelean. But whatever things have been properly said by each of those sects, inculcating justice and devout knowledge, this whole selection I call philosophy." Φιλοσοφίαν δέ, οὐ τὴν Στωϊκὴν λέγω, οὐδὲ τὴν Πλατωνικήν, ἢ τὴν Ἐπικούρειόν τε καὶ Ἀριστοτελικήν· ἀλλ' ὅσα εἴρηται παρ' ἑκάστῃ τῶν αἱρέσεων τούτων καλῶς, δικαιοσύνην μετ' εὐσεβοῦς ἐπιστήμης ἐκδιδάσκοντα, τοῦτο σύμπαν τὸ ἐκλεκτικὸν φιλοσοφίαν φημί. Stromm. Lib. I. p. 288.

whom I mentioned before; and indeed, for the
same reason, namely, for his having so industriously
and speciously marked out a seeming conformity
between two works, if I may so call them, both of
which they so highly reverenced.

The writings of Philo came the more strongly
recommended to these men, because the method
of interpretation, which he has adopted, may be as
commodiously applied by Christians to reconcile
the principles of Plato and the doctrines of the
Gospel, as it was by Philo to explain the contents
of the Old Testament by the same principles.

First, there are to be found in the writings of
many of the fathers of the Christian Church evident traces of the opinion, that the heathens derived all the principles of their knowledge from the
sacred Scriptures; and even that the wildest stories
of their mythology originated from the same source.
Thus, in *the Address to the Greeks*[3], attributed to
Justin Martyr, the author boldly asserts, that Or- p. 15. [B. § 14.
pheus, and Homer, and Solon, the legislator of the *ed. Otto.*]
Athenians, and Pythagoras, and Plato, and some
others, received great assistance from the writings
of Moses, ἐκ τῆς Μωυσέως ἱστορίας ὠφεληθέντες.
He affirms, that hence they derived the knowledge

But though the followers of the Eclectic philosophy professed
to select the truth from the doctrines of the several sects; yet
the authority of Plato, in their estimation, far surpassed that of
any other, and the bulk of their tenets concerning God and the
human soul was composed of his doctrines.

[3] Though there is reason to doubt whether this address
was really the work of Justin, it serves to shew, in conjunction
with the other quotations, that this opinion prevailed among
the early Christians.

of the unity of God, and some of the mysteries of the divine nature. He maintained, that Plato, in the beginning of the *Timæus*, in describing the principle of existence, obscurely alluded to the appellation which the supreme Being assumed to himself in the book of Genesis; but that he varied the form of expression, in order to evade the censure of the court of Areopagus: that when he speaks of an ancient account, he means the law of Moses[4]: that when he mentions men beloved of God, he thinks of Moses and the other prophets, from whose writings he learned the doctrine of a future judgment[5]: that when he made εἶδος, 'specific form,' the third principle after God and matter, he was led to the use of the expression by a passage in the writings of Moses, which, for the want of an enlightened instructor, he did not correctly understand: "Look, that thou make them after the pattern which was shewed thee in the Mount." And again, "According to all that I shew thee, after the pattern of the tabernacle and the pattern of all the instruments, even so shall ye make it[6]." Plato, says he, having met with these passages, supposed that some separate specific form existed, before

---

[4] Ἐνταῦθα ὁ Πλάτων σαφῶς καὶ φανερῶς τὸν παλαιὸν λόγον Μωϋσέως ὀνομάζει νόμον, τοῦ μὲν ὀνόματος Μωϋσέως, φόβῳ τοῦ κωνείου, μεμνῆσθαι δεδιώς. p. 24 [B].

[5] Ἄνδρας δὲ τίνας ἑτέρους τῷ Θεῷ φίλους εἶναι νομίζει, εἰ μὴ Μωϋσέα καὶ τοὺς λοιποὺς προφήτας; ὧν ταῖς προφητείαις ἐντυχὼν, καὶ τὸν περὶ κρίσεως παρ' αὐτῶν μεμαθηκὼς λόγον, ἐν τῷ πρώτῳ τῆς Πολιτείας λόγῳ οὕτω προαναφωνεῖ, p. 24 [E].

[6] Πλάτων δὲ μετὰ τὸν Θεὸν καὶ τὴν ὕλην τὸ εἶδος τρίτην ἀρχὴν εἶναι λέγων, καὶ [οὐκ l. Otto] ἀλλόθεν πόθεν ἀλλὰ παρὰ Μωϋσέως τὴν πρόφασιν εἰληφὼς φαίνεται, τὸ μὲν τοῦ εἴδους ὄνομα ἀπὸ τῶν

what is the object of the senses; which form he also often calls the pattern of the things that were made[7]. He then proceeds to point out the mistakes into which Plato fell in reading the Mosaical account of the Creation, and the manner in which he was led by those mistakes to imagine an intelligible world, and other opinions that appear in the Timæus. It is unnecessary to give a minute detail of these things, and of the allusion which, in the second Apology for Christians, Justin states the Philosopher to make to the shape of the cross, the knowledge of which he is supposed to have obtained from the story of the brazen serpent in the history of Moses. [Apolog. i. § 60, p. 92.]

In his *Dialogue* with Trypho the Jew he asserts, that the devil formed many of the mythological stories of the Greeks in imitation of the several circumstances foretold of Jesus Christ; in the same manner as the magicians of Egypt imitated the miracles that were performed by Moses. One instance of this is Bacchus, the son of Jupiter, who, having been torn to pieces, after his death rose again and ascended into heaven; whose mysteries also are celebrated with wine. Another instance is Æsculapius, who is represented as curing diseases [p. 294 [D.]]

Μωϋσέως μεμαθηκὼς ῥητῶν, οὐ διδαχθεὶς δὲ τηνικαῦτα παρὰ τῶν εἰδότων ὅτι οὐδὲν ἐκτὸς μυστικῆς θεωρίας τῶν ἀπὸ Μωϋσέως εἰρημένων σαφῶς γιγνώσκειν ἐστὶ δυνατόν. Γέγραφε γὰρ Μωϋσῆς ὡς τοῦ Θεοῦ περὶ τῆς σκηνῆς πρὸς αὐτὸν εἰρηκότος οὕτως, κ.τ.λ. p. 28. [D. § 29. p. 98.]

[7] Τούτοις οὖν ἐντυχὼν ὁ Πλάτων καὶ οὐ μετὰ τῆς προσηκούσης θεωρίας δεξάμενος τὰ γεγραμμένα ῥητὰ, ᾠήθη εἶδός τι χωριστὸν προϋπάρχειν τοῦ αἰσθητοῦ· ὃ καὶ παράδειγμα τῶν γενομένων ὀνομάζει πολλάκις. p. 29 [A].

[*Apolog.* i. c. 22: *Dial. cum Tryph.* c. 67. p. 296. [B. § 70.]

and raising the dead. Again, we hear of Perseus, who was born of a virgin. Again, when the Persians say that Mithras was born of a rock, they are supposed to have taken the idea from the book of the prophet Daniel, where the kingdom of God is prefigured by a stone cut out of a rock without hands.

p. 46.

Clemens Alexandrinus, in his *Admonition to the Gentiles*, expostulates with Plato, and asks him whence arose his conjecture about truth and genuine piety. I know your teachers, says he, though you may wish to conceal them. You are indebted to the Hebrews for such of your laws as are true, and for your opinion of God[8]. To the same origin he refers the knowledge which Xenophon had attained of the Supreme Being[9].

In the first book of his *Stromata* he gives an instance of a law which, he says, Plato borrowed from the Hebrews; wherein he orders every one to abstain from the water of his neighbour, till he has tried every method, without success, of procuring water in his own possessions[10]. In page

[§ xv. p. 358. ed. *Potter*.]

---

[8] Πόθεν, ὦ Πλάτων, ἀλήθειαν αἰνίττῃ; πόθεν ἡ τῶν λόγων ἄφθονος χορηγία τὴν θεοσέβειαν μαντεύεται;—οἶδά σου τοὺς διδασκάλους, κἂν ἀποκρύπτειν ἐθέλῃς—νόμους, ὅσοι ἀληθεῖς, καὶ δόξαν τὴν τοῦ θεοῦ, παρ' αὐτῶν ὠφέλησαι τῶν 'Εβραίων: [p. 60. ed. Pott. § 70.]

[9] Πόθεν ἄρα ὁ τοῦ Γρύλλου σοφίζεται; ἢ δηλαδὴ παρὰ τῆς προφήτιδος τῆς 'Εβραίων θεσπιζούσης ὧδε πως; [*Ibid.* § 71.]

[10] Ἐν γοῦν τοῖς Νόμοις ὁ ἐξ 'Εβραίων φιλόσοφος Πλάτων κελεύει τοὺς γεωργοὺς μὴ ἐπαρδεῦσαι μηδὲ λαμβάνειν ὕδωρ παρ' ἑτέρων, ἐὰν μὴ πρότερον ὀρύξαντες παρ' αὐτῶν ἄχρι τῆς παρθενίου καλουμένης, ἄνυδρον εὕρωσι τὴν γῆν: p. 274. [p. 321. *ed. Potter.*]

[11] Φιλοσοφία δὲ οὐκ ἀπεστάλη ὑπὸ Κυρίου· ἀλλ' ἦλθε, φησὶ, κλαπεῖσα, ἢ παρὰ κλέπτου δοθεῖσα· εἴτ' οὖν δύναμις ἢ ἄγγελος μαθών τι τῆς ἀληθείας καὶ μὴ καταμείνας ἐν αὐτῇ, ταῦτα ἐνέπνευσε καὶ

104 304, he says that Numa was a Pythagorean; but that it was in consequence of what he learned from Moses, that he prohibited the Romans from making an image of God. In page 309 is quoted, from [§ vii. p. 366. ed. Potter.] the Gospel of St John, the saying of our Saviour, [S. John x. 8.] that all before him were thieves and robbers. This some men applied to the philosophers, to whom the[11] arch-apostate surreptitiously communicated detached portions of divine wisdom. Yet, says Clemens, this philosophy, stolen as it were by Prometheus, retained a little fire emitting some useful light, a faint resemblance of divine wisdom. The Grecian philosophers, who lived before the coming of our Lord, may indeed be called thieves and robbers, for having, without acknowledging it, taken portions of truth from the Hebrew prophets, and appropriating them, as if they were their own doctrines[12]. He produces the authority of Aristobulus to prove that Plato was guided by the law of 105 the Jews[13]. He quotes the following passage from Numenius, a Pythagorean philosopher: What is Plato but Moses speaking the Attic language[14]?

κλέψας ἐδίδαξεν. p. 310. [§ 17, p. 366.]

[12] Ἔστιν οὖν κἂν φιλοσοφίᾳ τῇ κλαπείσῃ, καθάπερ ὑπὸ Προμηθέως, πῦρ ὀλίγον εἰς φῶς ἐπιτήδειον χρησίμως ζωπυρούμενον, ἴχνος τι σοφίας καὶ κίνησις παρὰ Θεοῦ· ταῦτα δ᾽ ἂν εἶεν κλέπται καὶ λῃσταὶ οἱ παρ᾽ Ἕλλησι φιλόσοφοι, καὶ πρὸ τῆς τοῦ Κυρίου παρουσίας παρὰ τῶν Ἑβραϊκῶν προφητῶν μέρη τῆς ἀληθείας οὐ κατ᾽ ἐπίγνωσιν λαβόντες, ἀλλ᾽ ὡς ἴδια σφετερισάμενοι δόγματα. p. 312. [§ 17, p. 369.]

[13] Κατηκολούθηκε δὲ καὶ ὁ Πλάτων τῇ καθ᾽ ἡμᾶς νομοθεσίᾳ, καὶ φανερός ἐστι περιεργασάμενος ἕκαστα τῶν ἐν αὐτῇ λεγομένων, p. 342, [p. 411.]

[14] Τί γάρ ἐστι Πλάτων, ἢ Μωϋσῆς ἀττικίζων; p. 342, [§ 22, p. 411.]

That Plato was assisted by the writings of Moses, when he composed his treatise on Laws, is again asserted (p. 349). In the second book (p. 367) he says, that the fable of Minos associating with Jupiter was invented by some who had heard that God had conversed with Moses, as a man converses with his friend.

I will not stop to remark the many conformities and resemblances which he has pointed out in the moral injunctions and observations of the Gentile philosophers and the inspired writers, particularly in the fourth book of his *Stromata*. Nor will I dwell upon what he says at the end of that book, that the Hyperborean and Arimaspian cities, the Elysian fields, and the Republic of Plato, are images (εἰκόνας) of the church, the heavenly Jerusalem. In the fifth book, p. 580, after mentioning some doctrines of Pythagoras, Socrates, and Plato, he affirms that they were derived from Moses[15]. In the 592d and the following pages, he enumerates many doctrines in confirmation of the same position concerning Plato. In p. 595, he alleges the authority of Aristobulus, that the Peripatetic philosophy was taken from the law of Moses. I shall conclude this topic with the following passage:

Καὶ τὸ σύνολον, Πυθαγόρας καὶ Σωκράτης καὶ Πλάτων λέγοντες ἀκούειν φωνῆς Θεοῦ, τὴν κατασκευὴν τῶν ὅλων θεωροῦντες ἀκριβῶς ὑπὸ Θεοῦ γεγονυῖαν

---

[15] Παρὰ Μωϋσέως τοιαῦτα φιλοσοφήσαντες οἱ τῶν Ἑλλήνων ἄκροι.

[16] Δύο δὲ παρειλήφαμεν Κέλσους γεγονέναι Ἐπικουρείους· τὸν μὲν πρότερον κατὰ Νέρωνα· τοῦτον δὲ κατὰ Ἀδριανὸν καὶ κατωτέρω.

καὶ συνεχομένην ἀδιαλείπτως· ἀκηκόασι γὰρ τοῦ Μωϋσέως λέγοντος, Εἶπε καὶ ἐγένετο.

Secondly, these sentiments naturally led those who entertained them to regard with a favourable disposition the writings of Philo, in which the plan is laboriously pursued of reconciling Divine Revelation and Pagan philosophy, and of expounding Scripture history upon heathen principles.

Origen, in the beginning of his *treatise against Celsus*, being desirous of giving his readers some idea of the qualities of his antagonist, and of the time in which he lived, says, We are told that there were two men, Epicureans, of the name of Celsus; the first in the time of Nero, but this in the time of Adrian and later [16]. Now, whatever practices Celsus really observed and objected to in the Christians, may fairly be presumed to have been of some duration and extent in his time; particularly if the charges were avowed and defended by the Apologist. One of the things, which Origen states him to impute to the Christians is, that they, in conjunction with the Jews, adopted allegorical explanations of the transactions recorded in the Books of Moses [17]. Origen supposes that Celsus referred to the works of Philo, and of some still more ancient, such as Aristobulus; and concludes, that he had never read those works himself, but had only heard that there were writings which contained allegorical

---

Lib. I. p. 8.
[17] Φησὶν, ὅτι καὶ Ἰουδαίων καὶ Χριστιανῶν οἱ ἐπιεικέστεροι ταῦτ' ἀλληγοροῦσι. Lib. IV. p. 196.

explanations of the law; otherwise he would not have spoken in so contemptuous a manner of such valuable compositions [18].

These instances seem to me to prove that the writings of Philo, and the allegorical mode of interpretation adopted by him, were in high estimation among Christians very early in the second century at the latest. The works of the Fathers of the Church in that age, particularly among the Greeks, abound in imitations, allusions, and direct references to him.

[§ v. p. 333. ed. Potter.] Clemens Alexandrinus, (*Strom.* Lib. i. p. 284.) discoursing about heavenly wisdom and philosophy, undertakes to confirm his reasonings by the testimony of Scripture. For this purpose he introduces the allegorical interpretation of Abraham, Sarah, and Agar, which interpretation he supports by the authority of Philo, and then pursues the same train of thought through Rebecca, Jacob, [Lib. i. cap. 5. [§ 21, p. 110.]] and Thamar. In like manner in his Παιδαγωγός he allegorizes the characters and story of Isaac, Rebecca, and Abimelech. In the same style he interprets the command of Moses to abstain from the flesh of swine, the eagle, &c. which he makes to signify a prohibition from voluptuousness and [§ viii. p. 677.] rapacity (*Strom.* Lib. v. p. 571). Thus also he ex- [ibid. p. 678.] plains (p. 572) Joseph in his coat of many colours

---

[18] Δοκεῖ δέ μοι καὶ ἀκηκοέναι, ὅτι ἐστὶ συγγράμματα περιέχοντα τὰς τοῦ νόμου ἀλληγορίας· ἅπερ εἰ ἀνεγνώκει, οὐκ ἂν ἔλεγεν, αἱ γοῦν δοκοῦσαι περὶ αὐτῶν ἀλληγορίαι γεγράφθαι, πόλυ τῶν μύθων αἰσχίους εἰσὶ καὶ ἀτοπώτεραι, τὰ μηδαμῇ μηδαμῶς ἁρμοσθῆναι δυνάμενα, θαυμαστῇ τινι καὶ παντάπασιν ἀναισθήτῳ μωρίᾳ συνάπτουσαι. ἔοικε δὲ περὶ τῶν Φίλωνος συγγραμμάτων ταῦτα λέγειν, ἢ καὶ τῶν

The Fathers of the Christian Church.

to signify a man endued with various knowledge.
In p. 583, the three days which Abraham spent [§ xi. p. 690.] in going to the place where he was to sacrifice his son, are made to signify the degrees by which a man advances to the knowledge of spiritual things. And in p. 574, he bestows high encomiums upon [§ ix. p. 679.] the utility and dignity of these allegories, and the interpretations of them.

Theophilus, in his second book of *Autolycus*, [§ 13 foll.] p. 94 *foll.* partly with hints taken from Philo, partly with additions of his own, to make the whole apply to Christianity, deduces a variety of allusions to the great mysteries of religion, the nature of God, the doctrine of the Trinity, the condition of man, and the dispensations of Providence, from the number of days employed in the creation of the world, the portion of them which preceded the creation of the luminaries of heaven, and the different productions of the several days.

I think I have now incontrovertibly established these two facts.

First, That the early Christians entertained the opinion that the philosophical principles and mythological stories of Pagan antiquity were derived either immediately or circuitously from the books of the Old Testament.

Secondly, That the allegorical writings of Philo

ἔτι ἀρχαιοτέρων, ὁποῖά ἐστι τὰ Ἀριστοβούλου. στοχάζομαι δὲ τὸν Κέλσον μὴ ἀνεγνωκέναι τὰ βιβλία, ἐπεὶ πολλαχοῦ οὕτως ἐπιτετεῦχθαί μοι φαίνεται, ὥστε αἱρεθῆναι ἂν καὶ τοὺς ἐν Ἕλλησι φιλοσοφοῦντας ἀπὸ τῶν λεγομένων· ἐν οἷς οὐ μόνον ἡ φράσις ἐξήσκηται ἀλλὰ καὶ νοήματα καὶ δόγματα καὶ ἡ χρῆσις τῶν ὡς οἴεται ἀπὸ τῶν γραφῶν μύθων ὁ Κέλσος, p. 198.

were in high estimation among the same people, and that the principles of interpretation which he had adopted were received as just and wise.

I shall now proceed to enquire into the effects which these two opinions conjointly produced in the reasonings of the Christians of the second century.

The first effect which I shall point out is this. We saw that Philo by an allegorical mode of interpretation explained the things, persons, and transactions, recorded in the Old Testament, to signify moral and intellectual qualities and operations. The Fathers of the Christian Church proceeded farther, and again converted those qualities and operations, with the supposed emblematic things, persons, and transactions, into other persons and transactions under the Gospel covenant.

Because in the *Timæus* of Plato the Creator is said to have used an ideal world as a pattern when he formed the present sensible one, Philo also, when he commented upon the Mosaical account of the creation, and applied to it the principles of Plato, represented the Supreme Being as forming within himself a plan of the work which he was about to accomplish. This plan, he says, was nothing else but the reason or reasoning of God, in the same manner as the plan of a city, formed by an architect, is the reasoning of that architect. Because the arrangement of this plan of course preceded the creation of the things which were to be formed according to it, he calls it the first-born (πρωτότοκος), by which word he expresses likewise the difference of its nature from that of external things, since it was the natural production of the divine intellect by a reflex act, if we may so express it. In other parts of his works he makes several things, persons, and actions, emblematically representative of the divine wisdom and its dealings with men. Because St John has called Christ ὁ λόγος, and he is elsewhere styled πρωτότοκος, it has been concluded that all which Philo has said of what he calls ὁ λόγος, is expressive of Christ in a literal sense.

Philo asserted that the two Cherubim over the mercy-seat were intended to signify the creative and governing powers of God. The creative power is said by Justin Martyr to be Christ, and is called by him a certain rational power, which God begat of himself in the beginning, before all created beings[19]. In his second *Apology for the Christians*, he calls the author of our salvation the reason, of which the whole human race partakes; and asserts, that they who lived according to reason are Christians, even though they were esteemed Atheists; as among the Greeks Socrates and Heraclitus, and such as were like them[20].

In like manner Athenagoras, stating the eternity of the son of God, and his consubstantiality with the father, says, I will tell you in short what

[19] Ἀρχὴν πρὸ πάντων τῶν κτισμάτων ὁ Θεὸς γεγέννηκε δύναμίν τινα ἐξ ἑαυτοῦ λογικήν: p. 284 [A. *Dialog. c. Tryph.* § 61.]

[20] Λόγον ὄντα, οὗ πᾶν γένος ἀνθρώπων μέτεσχε· καὶ οἱ μετὰ λόγου βιώσαντες Χριστιανοί εἰσι, κἂν ἄθεοι ἐνομίσθησαν· οἷον ἐν Ἕλλησι μὲν Σωκράτης καὶ Ἡράκλειτος καὶ οἱ ὅμοιοι αὐτοῖς: p. 83, [D. *Apol.* I. § 46.]

his being a son means: That he was the first production of the father, not as a thing that was made; for God, being an eternal mind, from the beginning had reason in himself, being eternally reasonable [21].

Theophilus, in the second book of his *Address to Autolycus*, explains in the same manner the λόγος as being always resident in the heart of God: for, before any thing was made, God had him as his counsellor, being his own mind and intellect. And when God willed to make whatever he counselled, he begat this *prophoric logos*, the first-born of all creation [22].

Tertullian, in his *Treatise against Hermogenes*, seems to pursue the same idea. Speaking of the nature of wisdom, he says, [23] When he perceived it necessary for the works of the world, he immediately establishes it and generates it in himself—Wisdom was born and established as soon as God began to dispose himself to set in order the works of the world—Though he had been about to make it of matter, he had before made it in wisdom, by meditating and arranging—He afterwards sets

---

[21] 'Ο παῖς τί βούλεται, ἐρῶ διὰ βραχέων· πρῶτον γέννημα εἶναι τῷ πατρί, οὐχ ὡς γενόμενον· ἐξ ἀρχῆς γὰρ ὁ Θεὸς, νοῦς ἀΐδιος ὤν, εἶχεν αὐτὸς ἐν ἑαυτῷ τὸν λόγον, ἀϊδίως λογικὸς ὤν. [*Supplic. pro Christian.* § 10.]

[22] Ἀλήθεια διηγεῖται τὸν λόγον, τὸν ὄντα διαπαντὸς ἐνδιάθετον ἐν καρδίᾳ Θεοῦ. πρὸ γάρ τι γίγνεσθαι, τοῦτον εἶχε σύμβουλον, ἑαυτοῦ νοῦν, καὶ φρόνησιν ὄντα· ὁπότε δὲ ἠθέλησεν ὁ Θεὸς ποιῆσαι ὅσα ἐβουλεύσατο, τοῦτον τὸν λόγον ἐγέννησε προφορικὸν, πρωτότοκον πάσης κτίσεως: P. 100, *Ed. Paris.* 1636. fo. [Ch. x.]

[23] Denique ut necessariam sensit ad opera mundi, statim eam condit et generat in semetipso—Sophia scilicet ejus exinde

forth this order in a more distinct manner. Wisdom was first established. After that was sent forth the word, by which all things were made, and without which nothing was made. In this passage the author evidently meant by *sophia*, *wisdom*, the internal conception, and by *sermo*, *word*, the external expression or command. Athenagoras has expressed something of the same kind, though not exactly in the same manner: the son of God is the *logos* of the father in idea and energy [24].

Upon this order Tertullian enlarges in his *Treatise against Praxeas*. Before all things God was alone, being to himself both world, and place, and all things. Now he is said to have been alone, because there was nothing externally beside him. Yet he was not even then alone; for he had with him what he had in himself, namely, his own reason. Even God is reasonable, and reason was in him first, and so all things were by him.— Although God had not yet sent forth his word, he had it within himself with and in his reason, by secretly considering and arranging with him-

---

nata et condita, ex quo in sensu Dei ad opera mundi disponenda cœpit agitari, p. 416. Tertullian, contrary to some other of the Fathers, reprobated refinements upon the word Ἀρχή. "Principium sive initium inceptionis est verbum non alicujus substantiæ nomen—Etiam ex materia facturus fuisset, ante in sophia cogitando et disponendo jam fecerat.—Primo sophiam conditam initium viarum in opera ejus: dehinc et sermonem prolatum, per quem omnia facta sunt, et sine quo factum est nihil." [p. 275, *ed. Rigalt. Paris.* 1634.]

[24] Ἐστὶν ὁ υἱὸς τοῦ Θεοῦ λόγος τοῦ πατρὸς ἐν ἰδέᾳ καὶ ἐνεργείᾳ. [*Supplic. pro Christ.* § 10.]

self what afterwards he was about to utter by the word [25]. This he proposes to illustrate by what takes place in man, who was made after the image of God, and has also reason in himself. Whenever he thinks, he speaks within himself, has a collocutor, and holds a conference with his reason [26]. Thus, says he to his adversary, there is in you a kind of secondary speech, by which you speak in thinking, and by which you think in speaking. Your very discoursing faculty becomes another person. How much more fully does this take place in God?

Tertullian seems to have been aware that the wisdom and word of God, according to his explanation, might be taken for a quality or an act. He therefore supposes his opponent to ask, if he maintained the word to be a substance; to which question he answers decidedly in the affirmative. In reply to this his adversary is made to object, that a word is something void, empty, and incor-

[25] Ante omnia enim Deus erat solus, ipse sibi et mundus et locus et omnia. Solus autem, quia nihil aliud extrinsecus præter illum. Ceterum ne tunc quidem solus; habebat enim secum, quam habebat in semetipso, rationem suam scilicet. Rationalis etiam Deus, et ratio in ipso prius: et ita ab ipso omnia—Etsi Deus nondum sermonem suum miserat, proinde eum cum ipsa et in ipsa ratione intra semetipsum habebat, tacite cogitando et disponendo secum, quæ per sermonem mox erat dicturus. p. 845. [p. 637, A, B *ed. Rigalt.*]

[26] Ita secundus quodammodo in te est sermo, per quem loqueris cogitando, et per quem cogitas loquendo. Ipse sermo alius est. Quanto ergo plenius hoc agitur in Deo? p. 846. [*Ib.* D.]

[27] Ergo, inquis, das aliquam substantiam esse sermonem, spiritu et sophiæ traditione constructam? Plane—Quid est, dices, sermo, nisi vox et sonus vocis, et (sicut grammatici tradunt) aer offensus, intelligibilis auditu; ceterum, vacuum nescio

115 poreal, the mere voice and sound of the mouth, and, as grammarians call it, impelled air, intelligible by hearing. Our author therefore in support of his assertion advances the following reason: I say that nothing empty and void can come forth from God—and that what proceeded from so great a substance, and made such great substances, is not itself void of substance [27]. He afterwards proceeds to illustrate the mutual relation of the three persons of the Holy Trinity by the root, the tree, and its fruits; a fountain, a river, and a stream; the sun, a ray of light, and the apex of the ray.

116 We have seen, that, according to Philo, in order to assist the understandings of men, who were unable to contemplate God under the simple character of the one self-existent Being, he was represented as attended by two principal powers and attributes, and considered under the threefold character, as the principle of existence, the principle of wisdom and goodness, and the principle of

quid et inane et incorporale? At ego nihil dico de Deo inane et vacuum prodire potuisse, ut non de inani et vacuo prolatum; nec carere substantia, quod de tanta substantia processit, et tantas substantias fecit, [p. 638 D]. The language which Gazalius uses in speaking of the *Coran* is similar to this: Ipsum (Deum) præterea loqui, imperare, prohibere, promittere, minari, sermone æterno, antiquo, qui subsistat in essentia ipsius, nec similis sit sermoni creaturarum, quique non consistat voce, quæ oriatur e commotione æris, et collisione corporum, neque literis quæ conficiantur concursu labiorum, aut motione linguæ, et esse Alcoranum, Legem, Evangelium, et Psalterium, libros ab ipso demissos super Apostolos suos, et legi Alcoranum linguis, inscribi libris, reponi cordibus, ita tamen ut interim sit antiquus, subsistens in essentia Dei, nec obnoxius fiat separationi et divisioni. Pocock. *Spec. Hist. Arab.* p. 288.

108   *The Fathers of the Christian Church.*

power and authority. These were supposed by Christian writers to indicate the three persons of the Holy Trinity, revealed in the Gospel Dispensation. According to this doctrine, the second person is spoken of either as the [28] mind of the first, or as the [29] reasoning faculty of that mind, or as the [30] internal operation or production of that faculty, or as the [31] external expression of that production. [32] Athenagoras combines three of those senses together.

Hence Praxeas, perceiving, that by this mode of interpretation, personality was to be attributed

[28] Νοῦς καὶ λόγος τοῦ πατρὸς ὁ υἱὸς τοῦ Θεοῦ. Athenag. p. 10. [*Suppl. pro Chr.* § ix.] Ὅλος νοῦς, ὅλος φῶς πατρῷον. Clem. Alex. [*Stromm.* Lib. vii. cap. 2, p. 831.]

[29] Rationalis enim Deus, et ratio in ipso prius—quæ ratio sensus ipsius est. Tertullian, p. 845, [p. 637 B.]

[30] Sophia scilicet ipsius exinde nata et condita, ex quo in sensu Dei ad opera mundi disponenda coepit agitari. Tertull. p. 416. Cum ratione enim sua cogitans atque disponens sermonem, eam efficiebat, quam sermone tractabat, p. 845. Clemens Alexandrinus [*Stromm.* Lib. v. cap. 3, § 16, p. 654] having quoted John xvii., *I am the truth*, thus expatiates upon it: Ὁ δὲ λόγος τοῦ Θεοῦ, Ἐγώ, φησὶν, εἰμὶ ἡ ἀλήθεια. νῷ ἄρα θεωρητὸς ὁ λόγος· τοὺς δὲ ἀληθινοὺς, ἔφη, φιλοσόφους, τίνας λέγεις; τοὺς τῆς ἀληθείας, ἦν δ᾽ ἐγώ, φιλοθεάμονας. ἐν δὲ τῷ Φαίδρῳ (p. 247) περὶ ἀληθείας, ὡς ἰδέας λέγων ὁ Πλάτων δηλώσει. ἡ δὲ ἰδέα ἐννόημα τοῦ Θεοῦ· ὅπερ οἱ βάρβαροι λόγον εἰρήκασι τοῦ Θεοῦ.

[31] Cum dicit Deus, *Fiat lux;* hæc est nativitas perfecta sermonis. Tertullian, p. 846, [p. 638 B.]

[32] Νοῦς, λόγος, σοφία, υἱὸς τοῦ πατρὸς, p. 27 [§ x]. This mode of explaining the nature of the second and third persons of the Holy Trinity, led some of the principal sects among the Mahometans to deny the existence of the divine attributes; lest by admitting them they should seem to infringe the fundamental article of their faith, the simple unity of the Deity. The account of Abul Farajius is: "Quod ad Motazalas attinet, illud, de quo inter eos in universum convenit, hoc est, quod attributa æterna ab essentia Creatoris, qui supra omnia excelsus, amove-

18 to mere qualities, operations, and relations, maintained that the Trinity in the divine nature was not a Trinity of persons, but was intended to express the different offices and relations of the same identical Being. In consequence of this position he asserted, that God the Father himself descended into the womb of the Virgin; that he was born of her; that he suffered; in short, that he was Jesus Christ[33].

In all these cases it is highly necessary to observe the mode of reasoning which is adopted; and to distinguish between the general doctrine laid

ant, fugientes distinctionem personarum, quam constituunt Christiani." Poc. *Spec. Hist. Arab.* p. 18. Another author reasons in this manner upon the same principle: "Infidelitatis arguuntur Christiani, quod tria statuunt æterna; quid ergo de iis pronuntiandum, qui septem aut plura statuunt?" *Ib.* p. 216. Wasel, the founder of this class of sects, thus expresses himself upon the subject in general terms: " Quicunque asserit significatum aut attributum æternum, duos statuit Deos." *Ib.* By this language they meant nothing more, than to assert the simple and indivisible essence of the Deity, which, according to the metaphysical notions of those ages, would not be consistent with an acknowledgment of his attributes. For instance, when they denied the attribute of knowledge to the Deity, they affirmed, " Deum per essentiam suam scire, non per scientiam." That in this embarrassed mode of expressing themselves, they had an eye to the metaphysics, which then prevailed among Christians, seems evident from the following passage of Sharestanius: " Dicunt illi, qui se æquitatis assertores vocant, Deum excelsum unum esse essentia sua, nullam esse ei divisionem, nullum attributum, unum etiam operibus suis, nec socium ipsi esse, nec æternum alium præter essentiam ipsius, nec consortem in operibus ipsius, nec fieri posse, ut reperiantur duo æterna, atque hoc est unitatem asserere." *Ibid.*

[33] Ipsum dicit patrem descendisse in virginem, ipsum ex ea natum, ipsum passum, denique ipsum esse Jesum Christum. Tertull. *Adv. Praxeam.* p. 844, [p. 634 A].

down, and the explanations made use of to illustrate the nature of it. Thus the most approved writers of the second century rested upon the authority of the Scriptures, the general doctrine of the eternal generation of the Son of God, his unity with the Father, and his being the person by whom all things were made, and without whom nothing was made that was made. But when they proceeded to particular explanations of this general doctrine, they had little or no assistance from the Scriptures, if we except a few figurative passages, which they explained in a literal sense [34]. Their principal dependence was upon their own ingenuity and imagination, furnished with wrong conceptions of things and modes of reasoning, by their mistaking the principles and designs of Plato and Philo. This led them to explain the unity of the second person of the Holy Trinity with the first, by denominating the second the mind of the first, thus making a distinction between God the Father and his own mind, and assigning a separate personality to each; as if God the Father were any other than mind, or it were conceivable that any being should understand by an intellect which was personally different from it, and which of course possessed a separate consciousness. This led them to explain the eternity of the second person, by denominating him the reason of the first, who existed from eter-

---

[34] An obscure expression is a weak basis for an elaborate system. Critic. Obs. on VIth Book of the Æneid.

[35] Clemens Alexandrinus says, that the heads of the principal heresies of his time were born in the reign of the emperor

nity, and was always possessed of reason. Hence it was, that the second person is described to be the wisdom of the first, or that operation of the divine reason and that plan of proceeding which was laid in the divine intellect before all creation. Hence, likewise, the author of our salvation is asserted to have been literally that word which was projected from the Father of our Lord Jesus Christ, when he said, Let there be light, and there was light; which is termed by Tertullian, the perfect nativity of the word.

20 The orthodox writers of the second century seem to have differed from the heretics[35] not so much in their prime abstract principles and modes of reasoning, as in their superior reverence for the canonical Scriptures and the doctrines obviously contained in them, and their ready reference to them alone in confirmation of their tenets. The former steadily adhered to the doctrines of the Scriptures, but had recourse to peculiar principles and modes of reasoning, in order to explain and illustrate the nature of real beings, whose existence and general character are revealed in the word of God, and to make them appear consistent with the philosophical tenets or popular opinions of those to whom they wished to recommend them. Many of the heretics set out with similar principles and modes of reasoning; but instead of confining them

Adrian, and lived to the time of the elder Antoninus: περὶ τοὺς Ἀδριανοῦ τοῦ Βασιλέως χρόνους οἱ τὰς αἱρέσεις ἐπινοήσαντες γεγόνασι, καὶ μέχρι γε τῆς Ἀντωνίνου τοῦ πρεσβυτέρου διέτειναν ἡλικίας. Stromm. Lib. viii. [p. 764, p. 898, Potter.]

to the explanation of acknowledged doctrines established upon the authority of the Scriptures, they gave up the reins to a wild imagination, and unchecked by authority, they proceeded as far as their fantastical principles and reasonings would carry them, in quest of new and unauthorized doctrines and imaginary personages.

I shall endeavour to illustrate what is here asserted, by a passage in that treatise of Tertullian, to which I have so often referred. Tertullian, having advanced what has been already stated concerning the reason and wisdom and word of God, seems to have been aware of the resemblance which his principles and reasonings bore to those that were maintained by Valentinus. He therefore undertook to obviate the objection, by pointing out the difference that was between them. Observe now in what he represents that difference to consist. It is not in the principles which he lays down; it is not in the reasonings and illustrations which he uses; but it is in the doctrines to which those prinples, reasonings, and illustrations are applied: *Hoc si qui putaverit me προβολὴν aliquam introducere, id est, prolationem rei alterius ex altera, quod facit Valentinus, alium atque alium Æonem de Æone producens; primo quidem dicam tibi, non ideo non utitur et veritas vocabulo isto et re ac sensu ejus, quia et hæresis utitur; immo hæresis potius ex veritate accepit, quod ad mendacium suum strueret. Prolatus est sermo Dei an non? Hic mecum gradum fige. Si prolatus est, cognosce probolam veritatis; et viderit hæresis, si quid de veritate imitata est. Jam nunc quæritur, quis quomodo utatur aliqua re et vocabulo ejus. Valentinus probolas suas discernit et separat ab auctore* 122 *et ita longe ab eo ponit, ut Æon patrem nesciat.— Apud nos autem solus filius patrem novit, et sinum patris ipse exposuit, et omnia apud patrem audivit et vidit, etc.* p. 846.

What those doctrines of Valentinus were, may be seen at large in Irenæus. The fact seems to be, that Valentinus and other heretics, in the same manner as the orthodox, adopted erroneous principles, which led them into false doctrines. They learned at one time to speak of mind, as a person distinct from the principle of existence; at another time, to attribute substance and personality to reason; at another time, to wisdom; at another time, to the word expressive of power and authority. But they did not sufficiently attend to a very material circumstance, to which the orthodox paid more regard, that all those positions were originally advanced to explain established and well authenticated doctrines, and the nature of real personages. They began with them as first principles and unquestioned truths, and framed such doctrines as seemed to arise out of them. Thus they were induced to adopt the doctrine of a perfect Æon before all things, eternal, incomprehensible, invisible, and unbegotten. Considering mind, reason, wisdom, truth, life, &c. as distinct in their meaning, they attributed a distinct personality to each, and devised a series of Æons, projected one from another in a long course of succession.

123 We have seen that Plato maintained the spe-

cific forms to be the real entities. By these, Philo stated him to mean the mere motions of the mind. But the several sects of Gnostics considered them as real things, that had a proper and actual subsistence, and held that every species of sensible fleeting things had an ideal permanent representative. It was easy and natural for them, thus disposed, and in a great measure free from the restraints of the doctrines of the canonical Scriptures, to fall in with the Eastern philosophy, and to embrace a doctrine which admitted of an extensive list of Æons, such as man, church, thought, will, &c., each the chief of a particular order of beings similar to himself.

This primary derivation of the doctrines of the Gnostics from the philosophical opinions of Plato, is expressly affirmed by Irenæus, in which chapter it is stated that they also borrowed many of their notions from the theories of other philosophical sects, and from the poetic mythologies of ancient Greece. *Non solum quæ apud comicos posita sunt arguuntur, quasi propria proferentes; sed etiam quæ apud omnes, qui Deum ignorant, et qui dicuntur philosophi, sunt dicta, hæc congregant, et quasi centonem ex multis et pessimis panniculis consarcientes subtili eloquio sibi ipsis præparaverunt.* He says, indeed, that they affected to confirm their wild theories by Scripture; but it was by the most forced and arbitrary interpretations of it, by collecting detached expressions and names, and treating them as one continued narration, just as if a person should undertake to frame a story by tacking together verses

Adv. Hæres. l. ii. c. 19.

widely dispersed through the works of Homer. But, says he, when the Word, the Only-begotten, and Life, and Light, and Saviour, and Christ, and Son of God are proved to be one and the same Being, and it is shewn that this same person was made flesh for us, the fabric of their Ogdoad is dissolved; and, when this is dissolved, their whole hypothesis falls to the ground[36].

Clemens Alexandrinus also, in the third book of his *Stromata*, discourses upon the use which Epiphanes, Carpocrates, Marcion, and other heretics, made of the principles and doctrines of Plato, and other philosophers. He says, that Epiphanes was instructed by his father, Carpocrates, in the doctrines of Plato[37], some of which he had mistaken: that Marcion derived some improper notions from the same source, and that he made an unskilful use of others. He attributes some of the errors of Cassianus to too great an attention to Plato; and he quotes from the writings of some of those heretics the very expression in the *Parmenides*, ἓν ἦν τὰ πάντα,

[36] Ἑνὸς γὰρ τοῦ αὐτοῦ δεικνυμένου λόγου καὶ μονογενοῦς καὶ ζωῆς καὶ φῶτος καὶ σωτῆρος καὶ Χριστοῦ καὶ υἱοῦ Θεοῦ, καὶ τούτου αὐτοῦ σαρκωθέντος ὑπὲρ ἡμῶν, λέλυται ἡ τῆς Ὀγδοάδος σκηνοπηγία. ταύτης δὲ λελυμένης, διαπέπτωκεν αὐτῶν πᾶσα ἡ ὑπόθεσις. Irenæ. *adv. Hær.* Lib. I. p. 40.

[37] Ἐπαιδεύθη μὲν οὖν παρὰ τῷ πατρὶ τήν τε ἐγκύκλιον παιδείαν καὶ τὰ Πλάτωνος, p. 428. [p. 511.] Δοκεῖ δέ μοι καὶ τοῦ Πλάτωνος παρακηκοέναι ἐν τῇ πολιτείᾳ [φαμένου], p. 430, [514]. Οἱ φιλόσοφοι δέ, ὧν ἐμνήσθημεν (Πυθαγόρας τε καὶ Πλάτων) παρ' ὧν τὴν γένεσιν κακὴν εἶναι ἀσεβῶς ἐκμαθόντες οἱ ἀπὸ Μαρκίωνος, p. 431, [516]. Οὐκ ἀσαφῶς δεδεῖχθαι ἡμῖν νομίζω, τὰς ἀφορμὰς τῶν ξένων δογμάτων τὸν Μαρκίωνα παρὰ Πλάτωνος ἀχαρίστως τε καὶ ἀμαθῶς εἰληφέναι, p. 434, [520]. ἡγεῖται δὲ ὁ γενναῖος οὗτος Πλατωνικώτερον, p. 466, [553].

[r. 375 A.]

p. 466.—Tertullian calls Valentinus apostate, heretic, and Platonist. (*De Carne Christi*, cap. xx.) *Relucere ideis semina Gnostidæ et Valentininæ hæreseos. De Anima*, p. 322.

It would be easy to multiply passages from Tertullian and others, in support of what is here advanced. I will close this topic with one testimony from the writings of an author in the beginning of the next century; a testimony upon this subject as unexceptionable as any one that can be obtained. The author whom I mean is Plotinus; a man inferior to few in application, acuteness of genius, and profound knowledge of the various methods in which the men of those times interpreted the philosophical opinions of Plato, and applied them to subjects of theology.

The ninth book of his second *Ennead* was written professedly to discuss the doctrines of the Gnostics. After having examined some of their principal doctrines at large, he says, 'These things have been partly taken from Plato; but whatever new things they have introduced, in order to form their own system of philosophy, those are found to be destitute of truth[38].' He then produces one instance of this from the *Timæus*. Plato said, that as mind sees ideas in that which is a living being, the Creator devised that the universe should con-

[Timæus, p. 39. fin.]

---

[38] Ὅλως γὰρ αὐτοῖς τὰ μὲν παρὰ τοῦ Πλάτωνος εἴληπται· τὰ δὲ, ὅσα καινοτομοῦσιν, ἵνα ἰδίαν φιλοσοφίαν θῶνται, ταῦτα ἔξω τῆς ἀληθείας εὕρηται, p. 203 [F].

[39] Εἰπόντος γὰρ αὐτοῦ, ᾗπερ οὖν νοῦς ἐνούσας ἰδέας ἐν τῷ, ὃ ἔστι ζῷον, καθορᾷ, τοσαύτας καὶ ὁ τόδε ποιῶν τὸ πᾶν διενοήθη σχεῖν· οἱ δὲ, οὐ συνέντες, τὸν μὲν ἔλαβον ἐν ἡσυχίᾳ ἔχοντα ἐν αὐτῷ πάντα

tain as many. But the Gnostics, not understanding this, conceived one mind at rest, having in it all entities; another mind beholding what was in it; and a third mind devising[39]. He next shews in what manner their ideas of the corruption of matter, and the impurity of all terrestrial things, were derived from Plato's direction to abstract the thoughts, and to withdraw the mind as much as possible from the influence of the body. He again intimates, p. 215 [G.] that they were led to hate the nature of the body in consequence of having heard Plato[40] complain much of it, on account of its being so great an impediment to the soul.

127 . The conclusion, which I would draw from the whole of the topic, is this: First, that the original general principles, adopted by both the orthodox and the heretics of the second century, were the same, and that the latter differed from the former, chiefly in consequence of the more unrestrained and licentious use which they made of those principles. Secondly, that the chief of those principles were derived immediately from the mythological stories and the tenets of the philosophers of Greece, particularly of Plato.

I have been the more particular in this enquiry, because Mosheim, and after him Brucker, has asserted, that the Gnostic heresies were derived

---

τὰ ὄντα· τὸν δὲ νοῦν ἕτερον παρ' αὐτὸν θεωροῦντα, τὸν δὲ διανοούμενον, p. 204 [A.].

[40] Καίτοι εἰ καὶ μισεῖν αὐτοῖς ἐποίει τὴν τοῦ σώματος φύσιν, διότι ἀκηκόασι Πλάτωνος πολλὰ μεμψαμένου τῷ σώματι, οἷα ἐμπόδιον παρέχων [ἐμποδία παρέχει, Creuzer] τῇ ψυχῇ.

solely from the oriental philosophy. The real state of the case seems to me to be this:

First, The genuine doctrines of Plato, in many points, bear a strong resemblance to the oriental philosophy; whence indeed they were derived by Pythagoras and Plato. The same may be said of the mythologies of ancient Greece, which in a great measure originated from the same source.

Secondly, This resemblance was increased by the manner in which the philosophy of Plato was taught at Alexandria, when that city became a distinguished seat of learning.

Thirdly, It was customary for those who aspired to eminence in their profession, to affect a more profound knowledge of the sublime doctrines of philosophy relating to God and the human soul.128 For this purpose they were not satisfied with what Plato taught upon those subjects; but, after they had gone through the course of education in his school, they applied to the oriental philosophy, from which Plato himself drew. Clemens Alexandrinus enumerates the several masters under whom he himself studied. Among these one was from the east. Plotinus, who was himself a kind of second father of the later Platonists, undertook, though he failed to accomplish, a journey into the east, for the purpose of perfecting himself in the philosophy of those countries.

We may hence be able to account for the high pretensions to wisdom which the Gnostics advanced, and for the contempt with which they treated Plato and his followers, with whom they

Stromm. Lib. i. p. 274.
[p. 322.]

The Fathers of the Christian Church.

had set out in the pursuit of truth. They looked upon him as one who had made but very little progress in the ways of true knowledge, and was qualified to teach men only the first rudiments of science. But they arrogated to themselves the name of sages, who were initiated into the great mysteries of God and nature. This contemptuous treatment of Plato and his doctrines could not fail to produce a proportionable degree of animosity in the later Platonists, whose vanity was severely wounded by the arrogant pretensions of the Gnostics.

129   These patch-work systems of heresy (if I may be allowed to borrow the idea of Irenæus) will the less surprise us, if we recollect an opinion, which generally prevailed in that age, that most of the sects of Grecian and Barbarian philosophy contained severally some scattered portions of truth, which it was the business of a wise man to collect and combine in one consistent scheme [41].

While these general principles prevailed, as well among the orthodox Christians as among heretics, Ammonius Saccas, who was educated a Christian, established a school at Alexandria. Philosophy at this time had gained an undoubted

---

[41] This opinion is thus stated by Clemens Alexandrinus : ξύμπαντες οὖν ῞Ελληνές τε καὶ Βάρβαροι, ὅσοι τἀληθοῦς ὠρέχθησαν, οἱ μὲν οὐκ ὀλίγα, οἱ δὲ μέρος τι, εἴπερ ἄρα, τοῦ τῆς ἀληθείας λόγου ἔχοντες ἀναδειχθεῖεν—οὕτως οὖν ἥ τε βάρβαρος ἥ τε Ἑλληνικὴ φιλοσοφία, τὴν ἀΐδιον ἀλήθειαν σπαραγμόν τινα οὐ τῆς Διονύσου μυθολογίας, τῆς δὲ τοῦ Λόγου τοῦ ὄντος ἀεὶ Θεολογίας πεποίηται. ὁ δὲ τὰ διῃρημένα συνθεὶς αὖθις, καὶ ἑνοποιήσας τέλειον τὸν λόγον ἀκινδύνως εὖ ἴσθ' ὅτι κατόψεται τὴν ἀλήθειαν. Stromm. Lib. I. p. 298, [p. 349.]

ascendency in the church; and the nature of the situation, in which Ammonius was placed seemed to call upon him to support at once the character of divine revelation and human philosophy. As he left no writings behind him, we can judge of his abilities only from their effects, and the testimony of others. These unite in placing him in the most conspicuous point of view. In his endeavours to render more complete the agreement between the several stories of Pagan mythology, the tenets of the Grecian and Oriental philosophers, and the doctrines of the Gospel, he entirely changed the whole state of the question, effected a complete revolution in philosophy, and made no inconsiderable impression upon the Christian profession. By the refinements of his speculations and the copiousness and force of his eloquence, he seems to have exercised an almost uncontrollable influence over the minds of men in the personal discharge of his office as a public teacher. And from him sprung a sect, the members of which, for their learning and acutenesss, have been the admiration of great numbers in all succeeding ages.

130

Ammonius is said to have differed in principles from Clemens in the following respect. Clemens affirmed, that truth was dispersed in different portions through most of the stories of Pagan mythology and the several sects of philosophy; and that the great error of the heathens consisted principally in this, that each nation, party and sect, having but a portion of truth, and some of them a very small portion of it, persuaded themselves that they possessed the whole[42]. Whereas Ammonius is said to have affirmed, that each sect and party would be found to be possessed of all the most important doctrines of true religion, if their principles, tenets, and mythologies, were properly interpreted. This step alone was wanting in order to make the junction between Christianity and Paganism complete. If the point could be fully accomplished, it would follow of course that the school of Ammonius would be frequented by men of all parties who repaired to Alexandria for instruction in philosophy and religion. The event was answerable to the greatness of the undertaking, and the splendid abilities of the undertaker.

Before the time of Ammonius, Christian writers had for different purposes endeavoured to make out a conformity between their own profession and the traditions and principles of those to whom they addressed themselves. Sometimes they did this in order to mitigate the abhorrence in which they were held by their Pagan persecutors, and to convince them of the innocence and reasonableness of the doctrines which they taught and practised. At other times their views were more extensive and disinterested, and were directed to the conversion of those to whom their discourses were delivered. They represented to them, that the mythological traditions and philosophical speculations, which were so

---

[42] Αἱ τῆς φιλοσοφίας τῆς τε βαρβάρου τῆς τε Ἑλληνικῆς αἱρέσεις, ἑκάστη, ὅπερ ἔλαχεν, ὡς πᾶσαν αὐχεῖ τὴν ἀλήθειαν. *Stromm.* Lib. I. p. 298, [p. 349.]

highly esteemed by the Gentiles, were but faint and very imperfect copies of divine wisdom that was to be found only among Christians complete in all its parts, and with undiminished lustre. They exhorted them therefore to repair to the sacred volumes, where those celestial treasures are deposited, and to enrol themselves in that order of men who glory in professing and practising the most sublime truths and the purest morality, and in inculcating the same profession and practice upon others. Sometimes their object was to make philosophy appear respectable in the eyes of their fellow Christians, from a conviction that it tended to strengthen their intellectual powers, to enlarge their capacities, and refine their conceptions, and give them more just and comprehensive views of the ways of God in man. Perhaps also those good men were not quite free from some tincture of vanity in this respect. As they were undoubtedly ambitious of being reputed philosophers as well as Christians, they probably felt some pleasure in exalting their profession.

Yet all this while, Christianity, its doctrines, and language, seem to have engaged very little of the attention of Pagan philosophers. They saw no purposes of interest, ambition, or vanity, that were to be answered by concurring in those forced interpretations, in order to promote a seeming conformity. They were indeed often pressed by the Christian apologists with the gross impurities that were recorded in the histories of their gods; and the Stoics, whose system of religious faith comprehended them all, had given them a specimen of the excellent use that might be made of physical interpretations. Yet all those circumstances appear to have made but a slight impression upon their minds before the time of Ammonius; and they betray no symptoms of having even suspected that their popular mythologies, poetical fables, and philosophical tenets, contained either those express declarations of theological doctrines, or those obscure allusions to them, in which their successors so confidently affirmed that they every where most obviously abounded.

But when the reputation of Ammonius gave a consequence and dignity to the doctrines which he professed, the scene was suddenly changed. The Pagan philosophers seemed at once to be roused, as it were, from a profound sleep. A thick veil appeared to have been drawn from their eyes. Men of the most refined wit, the most acute genius, and the most extensive learning, thought it an employment worthy of their noblest faculties and attainments to search for the great mystery of revelation, the Trinity of Persons in the Divine Nature, among the doctrines and traditions of men. They tortured their invention a thousand ways in order to accomplish their purpose; and they did not disdain to use scriptural language and scriptural figures and illustrations in the prosecution of it. Now the withered arm was impiously lifted up against him who gave it strength. Now the Pagan ventured to enter into competition with the Christian concerning the purity of their respective moral precepts. Now he presumed to assail the authenticity of the revelation, by asserting that Christ and his disciples proclaimed nothing new concerning either the nature of God or the duty of man, but only set forth in a new form what was known to the world long before.

The most illustrious of the Pagan scholars of Ammonius was Plotinus. He stands eminently distinguished by the manner in which he applied the hypothesis and principles of his master to the decoration of the mythology and philosophy of Greece. The acuteness of his genius, his abstracted mode of reasoning and expression, and his unremitting application of metaphysical subtilties, gave a wonderful degree of reputation to his system.

> It seem'd
> For dignity compos'd and high exploit:
> But all was false and hollow[43].

If we refer to the detached original stories and reasonings which he undertook to illustrate and conjoin; if we attempt to explore the foundations of what, by the power, as it were, of his magic art, appeared in the eyes of some men to be a solid and stately building; we shall be surprised to discover that it is nothing more than the baseless fabric of a vision.

[43 Milton, *Paradise Lost*, Book II. v. 110.]

[44] Ἀρχέτυπον οἷον καὶ παράδειγμα εἰκόνος τούτου ὄντος καὶ δι' ἐκεῖνον ὄντος. *Enn.* III. Lib. ii. cap. 1. [p. 255 B.]

[45] Ἡ τοῦ νοῦ καὶ τοῦ ὄντος φύσις κόσμος ἐστὶν ὁ ἀληθινὸς καὶ πρῶτος. [*Ibid.* B.]

The writings of Plotinus are to be considered as philosophical lectures, in which he undertakes, not to investigate, but to prove and illustrate certain doctrines by a variety of arguments and statements. The principal of those doctrines, to which his chief attention is directed through all his works, is a trinity in the divine nature; (*Ennead* II. [p. 399.] Lib. IX. Cap. i. and elsewhere.) This doctrine, so conspicuous and important in the Christian dispensation, he endeavours to prove by abstract reasoning, to support by the authority of Plato, and to illustrate by mythological stories. He calls his three principles, the first, the good (τἀγαθόν) or the existing (τὸ ὂν), the second, mind (νοῦς), the third, soul (ψύχη). He says, that mind is the archetype and pattern of this world, which is the image of it, and which exists by means of it[44]; that the nature of mind and the existing is the true and first world[45]. Mind, having imparted something of itself to matter, made all things, itself remaining motionless and quiet. That which flowed from it was reason[46]. It was reason that gave harmony and an unity of composition to all things[47]. But this universe is not, like the intelligible one, mind and reason. It only partakes of mind and reason. Wherefore it stood in need of harmony by the concurrence of mind and necessity. The latter tends to defect and dis-

[46] Νοῦς τοίνυν δοὺς τι ἑαυτοῦ εἰς ὕλην, ἀτρεμὴς καὶ ἥσυχος τὰ πάντα εἰργάζετο· οὗτος δὲ ὁ λόγος, ἐκ νοῦ ῥυεὶς. Cap. 2, [p. 256 A.]

[47] Τοῦ δὲ λόγου ἐπ' αὐτοῖς τὴν ἁρμονίαν καὶ μίαν τὴν σύνταξιν εἰς τὰ ὅλα ποιουμένου. *Ibid.* [c.]

proportion; but mind controls necessity [48]. He again repeats this sentiment, that the reason or soul, which presides over this universe, is not, like that of the intelligible world, pure mind and soul, but suspended from the latter, and, as it were, an effulgence from both [49]. This reason therefore, though it proceeds from one mind and one life, each of them perfect, is neither one life nor one mind, nor every where perfect; and does not impart itself whole and entire to those things to which it imparts itself [50].

[Ennead. III. Lib. v. p. 292 c. foll.] In his treatise on the nature of Love, he makes use of these principles to explain the birth of that urchin, as related by Plato in his *Symposium*. There was, he says, a twofold Venus: one the daughter of Jupiter and Dione, the other the heavenly Venus or the divine soul, descended from Cœlus the first principle, but the immediate production of Cronus, mind, the second principle, without a mother, that is, without any communication with matter, and without any relation to marriage; as there is no marriage in heaven, every thing there being pure and unmixed. It is more immediately connected with mind than the light with the sun. This heavenly Venus, following

---

[48] Ἐστὶ γὰρ τὸ πᾶν τόδε οὐχ, ὥσπερ ἐκεῖ, νοῦς καὶ λόγος, ἀλλὰ μετέχον νοῦ καὶ λόγου· διὸ καὶ ἐδεήθη ἁρμονίας, συνελθόντος νοῦ καὶ ἀνάγκης. τῆς μὲν πρὸς τὸ χεῖρον ἑλκούσης καὶ εἰς ἀλογίαν φερούσης —ἄρχοντος δὲ νοῦ ὅμως ἀνάγκης. *Ibid.*

[49] Ἐστὶ τοίνυν οὗτος (ὁ λόγος) οὐκ ἄκρατος νοῦς, οὐδ' αὐτονοῦς, οὐδέ γε ψυχῆς καθαρᾶς τὸ γένος· ἠρτημένος δὲ ἐκείνης, καὶ οἷον ἔκλαμψις ἐξ ἀμφοῖν νοῦ καὶ ψυχῆς. [p. 267 D.]

[50] Ἥκων τοίνυν οὗτος ὁ λόγος ἐκ νοῦ ἑνὸς καὶ ζωῆς μιᾶς, πλή-

Cronus, or, if you please, his father Cœlus, associating with him and beloved by him, brought forth heavenly love. But the soul of this universe also has a love [p. 294 D.] attending her, who is concerned in marriages. This love was begotten at the birth of Venus, in the gardens of Jupiter, upon Πενία, *poverty*, by Πόρος, *abundance*. In this fable, he says, that Jupiter [p. 298 B.] does not mean the third principle, as it usually does, but the second, viz. mind. For Venus signifies the divine soul. Πόρος signifies the reason of all things: not abstract universal reason, or, as he expresses it, reason remaining in itself, but an effulgence from it, and mixed with Πενία, indefinite matter void of qualities[51]. Nectar, with which Πόρος is said to have been intoxicated, signifies divine wisdom, flowing into the soul at the birth of Venus. The gardens of Jupiter are the glory and splendor of the divine mind. (C. viii. ix. x). [pp. 298, 299.]

In the fifth *Ennead*, the first book, and the seventh chapter, he applies the story of Cronus or Saturn, Rhea, and Jupiter, to a similar purpose. Cronus, the wisest God, signifies the divine [p. 489 B.] intellect, which devours its own offspring[52]; that is, absorbs within itself the divine reasons, not suffer-

ρους ὄντος ἑκατέρου, οὐκ ἔστιν οὔτε ζώη μία, οὔτε νοῦς τις εἶς, οὔτε ἑκασταχοῦ πλήρης, οὐδὲ διδοὺς ἑαυτὸν οἶς δίδωσιν ὅλον τε καὶ πάντα. *Ibid.* [G].

[51] Ἐκ λόγου οὐ μείναντος ἐν αὐτῷ, ἀλλὰ μιχθέντος ἀοριστίᾳ. *Enn.* III. Lib. v. cap. 7, [p. 297 B.]

[52] The Stoics interpreted Cronus to signify time, his offspring days, months, and years, etc. "Κρόνος dicitur, qui est idem χρόνος, id est, spatium temporis. Saturnus autem est

ing them to sink into matter, and to be fostered by Rhea. From him, however, sprung Jupiter, the divine soul, the light and impression of the mind, revolving round it, and attached to it: a power too great to be unproductive.

In aid of this solemn trifling he had recourse to the philosophical principles of Plato. In the prosecution of his plan, he considers the *Parmenides*, the *Timæus*, and τὸ ἀγαθόν or universal good, and contemplates them as if they all treated the same subject in exactly the same point of view; though the *Parmenides* was intended to explain the phænomena of the universe, according to the principles of Parmenides, on the supposition of its having existed from eternity. Timæus, on the other hand, proceeds upon the supposition that the world was created, and undertakes to delineate the order in which that great work was performed, the relative dignity of the separate parts, and the ingredients of which they were severally composed. In neither of these treatises does Plato make himself absolutely responsible for the doctrines which are advanced in them. And in his dialogue concerning a Republic, he is not treating of the first and efficient cause,

appellatus, quod saturetur annis. Ex se enim natos comesse fingitur solitus, quia consumit ætas temporum spatia, annisque præteritis insaturabiliter expletur." Cic. *De Nat. Deor.* Lib. ii. cap. 25.

[53] Αὔταρκες ὂν αὐτῷ εἰς ἀγαθόν, οὐδὲν ἂν δέοιτο τῆς νοήσεως τῆς περὶ αὐτοῦ. *Enn.* VI. Lib. vii. cap. 38, [p. 730 A]. The terms in which he describes it, are not unlike the account, which Cicero gives of the Gods of Epicurus: "Nihil agit: nullis occupationibus est implicatus: nulla opera molitur: sua sapientia

but of the final cause. It is obvious how forced an interpretation it must be that aims at blending such inconsistencies in one system. But this is not all. The manner in which this scheme is conducted adds greatly to the confusion that necessarily arises from the nature of the scheme itself.

He affirms that the terms ἕν, ἓν πολλά, and ἓν καὶ πολλά in the *Parmenides* signify the three principles in the divine nature; and that τὸ ἀγα- [p. 490 B.] θόν, which I have shewn to signify the final cause, is equivalent to ἕν the first principle, (*Ennead* VI. [p. 731.] Lib. VII. C. xl. and elsewhere) the root, as it were, of the tree, (*Ennead* VI. Lib. VIII. C. xv. *Ennead* V. [p. 750 D, p. 617 C.] Lib. IV. C. i.) the first intelligible, a simple unit (*Ennead* V. Lib. II. C. i.) ungenerated and selfsuf- [p. 518.] ficient, not standing in need of intellect to complete its perfection [53]. Whereas the second principle, mind, which, he says, is the same as ἓν πολλά, requires the intelligible for the exercise of its powers and the fruition of its enjoyment, and of course for the perfection of its nature [54]. Mind has essence and intelligence, which are many. (*Ennead* VI. Lib. VII. C. xxxvii, [p. 728][55]). It is also all things, and therefore many. (*Ennead* III.

et virtute gaudet: habet exploratum fore se semper cum in maxumis tum in æternis voluptatibus." *De Nat. Deor.* I. 19.

[54] Ὁ μὲν γὰρ νοῦς τοῦ ἀγαθοῦ, τὸ δ᾽ ἀγαθὸν οὐ δεῖται ἐκείνου. *Enn.* III. Lib. viii. cap. 10, [p. 352 D]. Ὁρᾷ ὁ νοῦς ἐκεῖνον καὶ δεῖται αὐτοῦ μόνου· ἐκεῖνος δὲ τούτου οὐδέν. *Enn.* V. Lib. i. cap. 6, [p. 487 F]; Lib. iv. cap. 2, [p. 518].

[55] Δύο ὄντα τοῦτο τὸ ἓν ὁμοῦ νοῦς καὶ ὄν, καὶ νοῦν καὶ νοούμενον. ὁ μὲν νοῦς κατὰ τὸ νοεῖν· τὸ δὲ ὂν κατὰ τὸ νοούμενον. *Enn.* V. Lib. i. cap. 4, [p. 485 E].

130   *The Fathers of the Christian Church.*

[p. 273 B.]
[p. 560 A.]
Lib. III. C. iii.—*Ennead* V. Lib. IX. C. vi.) It is generated of the first principle by a reflex view of itself [56].

As mind is generated from the first principle by a reflex view, so it also, being at rest, out of 141 its essence produces soul. The soul, not indeed at rest but in motion, begat likewise an image. Looking at the principle whence it sprung, it was filled; and having proceeded to different and contrary motion, she generated an image of herself, sensation, and the nature which is in plants [57]. Soul is the reason of the mind, and an energy of it; as that is of the first principle. But the reason of the soul is obscure [58]. As the emitted reason is an image of the reason in the soul, so is the soul the image and reason of the mind; and it is all energy and life, which it sends forth for the subsistence of other things. One may be compared to the heat which resides in fire, the other to that which it communicates [59]. The soul, being one as subsisting in the divine nature, is also many

[56] Πῶς οὖν νοῦν γεννᾷ, ἢ ὅτι τῇ ἐπιστροφῇ πρὸς αὐτὸ ἑώρα. ἡ δὲ ὅρασις αὕτη νοῦς. *Enn.* v. Lib. i. cap. 7, [p. 488 A] : ὃν γὰρ τέλειον τῷ μηδὲν ζητεῖν μηδὲ ἔχειν, μηδὲ δεῖσθαι, οἷον ὑπερερρύη. καὶ τὸ ὑπερπλῆρες αὐτοῦ πεποίηκεν ἄλλο, τὸ δὲ γενόμενον εἰς αὐτὸ ἐπεστράφη καὶ ἐπληρώθη, καὶ ἐγένετο πρὸς αὐτὸ βλέπον. καὶ νοῦς οὗτος. καὶ ἡ μὲν προεκεῖνο [πρὸς ἐκεῖνο *l.* Creuzer] στάσις αὐτοῦ τὸ ὂν ἐποίησεν· ἡ δὲ πρὸς αὐτὸ θεὰ, τὸν νοῦν. ἐπεὶ οὖν ἔστι [ἔστη *l.* Creuz.] πρὸς αὐτὸ ἵνα ἴδῃ, ὁμοῦ νοῦς γίγνεται καὶ ὄν. *Enn.* v. Lib. ii. cap. 1, [p. 494 B].

[57] Οὕτως οὖν ὂν οἷον ἐκεῖνος, τὰ ὅμοια ποιεῖ, δύναμιν προχέας πολλήν. εἶδος δὲ καὶ τοῦτο αὐτοῦ, ὥσπερ αὐτὸ αὐτοῦ πρότερον προέχεε. Καὶ αὕτη ἐκ τῆς οὐσίας ἐνέργεια ψυχῆς [ψυχὴ *l.* Creuz.], τοῦτο μένοντος ἐκείνου γενομένη. καὶ γὰρ ὁ νοῦς μένοντος τοῦ πρὸ αὐτοῦ ἐγένετο. ἡ δὲ οὐ μένουσα ποιεῖ, ἀλλὰ κινηθεῖσα ἐγέννα εἴδωλον.

142 as consisting of the reasons of the things that are made⁶⁰.

She made all animals, breathing into them life: whatever the earth or the sea nourishes, and whatever are in the air or in heaven, the stars and the sun. She arranged this great heaven, and makes it revolve in regular order, being a nature different from the things which she arranges, and moves, and causes to live. When she communicates life to them, they come into being; when she quits them, they perish. Without her, matter is a dead carcass; but she flows into it, and enlightens it. As the rays of the sun, illuminating a dark cloud, make it shine, and give it an aspect of golden splendor, so also soul, entering into the body of heaven, gave it life and immortality.

Enn. v. Lib. i. c. 2. [p. 482 A., p. 483.]

It should seem that it would be a bold undertaking and an arduous task to reconcile this theory with the doctrines laid down in *Timæus*. In this theory mind and soul are stated to be the second and third principles, and to be co-

ἐκεῖ μὲν οὖν βλέπουσα ὅθεν ἐγένετο, πληροῦται. προελθοῦσα δὲ εἰς κίνησιν ἄλλην καὶ ἐναντίαν, γεννᾷ εἴδωλον αὐτῆς, αἴσθησιν καὶ φύσιν τὴν ἐν τοῖς φυτοῖς. *Ib.* [p. 494 c.]

⁵⁸ Ἡ ψυχὴ λόγος νοῦ, καὶ ἐνέργειά τις, ὥσπερ αὐτὸς ἐκείνου. ἀλλὰ ψυχῆς μὲν ἀμυδρὸς ὁ λόγος. *Enn.* v. Lib. i. cap. 6, [p. 487 F].

⁵⁹ Ἡ ψυχὴ—εἰκών τίς ἐστι νοῦ. οἷον λόγος ὁ ἐν προφορᾷ λόγου τοῦ ἐν ψυχῇ, οὕτω τοι καὶ αὐτὴ λόγος νοῦ. καί ἡ πᾶσα ἐνέργεια. καὶ ἣν προίεται ζωὴν εἰς ἄλλου ὑπόστασιν. οἷον πυρός, τὸ μὲν ἡ συνοῦσα θερμότης, ἡ δὲ ἣν παρέχει. *Enn.* v. Lib. i. cap. 3, [p. 484 B.]

⁶⁰ Τὸ δὲ ποιοῦν ἦν ψυχὴ, τοῦτο ἄρα πλῆθος ἕν. τί οὖν τὸ πλῆθος; οἱ λόγοι τῶν γιγνομένων. *Enn.* VI. Lib. ii. cap. 5, [p. 599 B].

MORGAN G

eternal and co-essential with the first principle, and to flow necessarily from it by a gradual process; that is, mind from the first principle, and soul from mind. Soul, in like manner, from the same necessity of its nature diffusing the emana- 143 tions of its essence through matter, and giving it form and life, constituted the visible world, with all that it contains. In the *Timæus* the three principles, as has been justly observed, are the Creator, Idea which is denominated the pattern, and Matter. Out of the two last the first is said by a voluntary and deliberate act (βουληθεὶς καὶ λογισάμενος) at the beginning of time to have made the universe, consisting of mind in soul and soul in body. But Plotinus was not discouraged by the difficulty, that would have deterred a less enterprizing genius; and he has shewn by the manner in which he surmounted it, that nothing is arduous to a sophist, who is indulged with an arbitrary assumption of abstract principles and ænigmatical interpretations. He says that Plato does not always appear to assert the same doctrines; so that it

61 Οὐ ταὐτὸν λέγων πανταχῇ φαίνεται, ἵνα ἄν τις ἐκ ῥᾳδίας τὸ τοῦ ἀνδρὸς βούλημα εἶδεν. *Enn.* IV. Lib. viii. cap. 1, [p. 469 B.] Cicero in his dialogue, *De Nat. Deor.* Lib. i. cap. 12, makes Velleius the Stoic bring the same charge of inconstancy of principles against Plato: *De Platonis inconstantia longum est dicere, etc.* The instances which he produces, are taken from the *Timæus* and the Books of *Laws*. If he had thought that the *Timæus* and the *Parmenides* treated precisely of the same subject, and that in both those dialogues Plato intended to convey his own sentiments; the strongest possible argument that could have been advanced, might have been obtained from a comparison of the different doctrines maintained in those two dialogues. For Velleius clearly perceived, that the positive

The Fathers of the Christian Church.   133

is not easy to ascertain his opinion [61]: that he
144 does but obscurely intimate, (ἠνιγμένος — αἰνιττόμενος. *Ennead* VI. Lib. II. Cap. xxii.), that mind [p. 614 A.]
sees ideas in the first principle, together with the
principal consequences deduced from it: that when
the production of mind or soul is mentioned, it is
not intended to signify a production in time, but
only to point out the order of causes [62]: that according to Plato mind sees ideas in the living,
which he calls also the intelligible: that by the
contemplation of those ideas is generated reason
or soul, which divides them into the several existing reasons or souls: that the universal soul was
not any where, and did not come any whither;
but body, being near it, partook of it: it was not
in body, nor does Plato say so; but body was in
it. Other souls proceed from it, and return to it;
but itself is always above, in that, whose nature is
existence. *Ennead* III. Lib. IX. Cap. i. ii.   [pp. 856, 857.]

145   If we consider the almost innumerable stories
of Pagan mythology, together with the various methods of relating and explaining them, we shall

creation of the world was taught in the *Timæus*. But Cicero
understood the principles of reasoning too well to put such an
objection into the mouth of any of his disputants, whom he
represents as the leading men of their several sects: *tres trium
disciplinarum principes*. It was incumbent upon Plato to preserve a consistency of principles and doctrines in the same discourse. But it was by no means necessary, that he should
maintain the same doctrines in explaining the physiology of
Parmenides and the cosmogony of Timæus.

[62] Ἐκποδὼν δὲ ἡμῖν ἔστω γένεσις ἡ ἐν χρόνῳ, τὸν λόγον περὶ
τῶν ἀεὶ ὄντων ποιουμένοις. τῷ δὲ λόγῳ τὴν γένεσιν προσάπτοντας
αὐτοῖς, αἰτίας καὶ τάξεως αὐτοῖς ἀποδώσει.   *Enn*. v. Lib. i. cap. 6,
[p. 487 c.]

G 2

readily see that it would not be difficult for so subtil a genius to cull something from them, which to those, who revered his authority, might seem to carry with it an air of probability, and to fall in with his favourite system.

The allegorical method of interpreting the Pagan mythology was attacked with great spirit and acuteness by Arnobius. The new theological mode of interpretation does not appear to have attracted his notice. He confines himself chiefly to the physical explanations, which were more ancient and general, though most of his observations are equally applicable to the other. One of the most obvious objections is, that both the accounts and interpretations of different authors are at great variance with each other. Among other instances he mentions the Muses, who, according to Mnaseas, were the daughters of Tellus and Cœlus. Other accounts made them the daughters of Jupiter and Memory, or Mind. Some said, that they were virgins;

[Adv. Nationes. Lib. iii. cap. 37, sqq.]

[63] [Nec defuerunt, qui scriberent Jovem, Junonem ac Minervam Penates existere, sine quibus vivere ac sapere nequeamus sed qui penitus nos regant ratione, colore ac spiritu. Ut videtis, et hic quoque nihil concinens dicitur, nihil una pronuntiatione finitur, nec est aliquid fidum, quo insistere mens possit veritati suæ proxima suspicione conjiciens.]

[64] From this account it should seem, that very little stress can be laid upon the following passage in Cudworth's *True Intellectual System*, p. 451. 'Nevertheless it may justly be suspected, as G. J. Vossius hath already observed, that there was yet some higher and more sacred mystery, in this Capitoline Trinity, aimed at; namely, a Trinity of divine Hypostases. For these three Roman or Capitoline Gods, were said to have been first brought into Italy out of Phrygia by the Trojans, but before that, into Phrygia by Dardanus, out of the Samothracian Island; and that within eight hundred years after the

others affirmed, that they were mothers. Ephorus said, that they were three in number; Mnaseas, that they were four; Myrtilus, that they were seven; Crates, that they were eight; Hesiod, that they were nine.

146 Again, concerning the Penates, Nigidius as- [Ib. c. 40,sqq.] serted, that they were Neptune and Apollo who encircled Troy with walls. The same man, in other places, mentions four kinds of Penates. Cæsius thinks, that they are Fortune, Ceres, Genius Jovialis; and Pales, a male, an attendant of Jupiter. Varro maintains, that neither their number, nor their names are known. The Tuscans affirm, that they are six males and six females. "Nor, says he, have there been wanting men who maintained that they are Jupiter, Juno, and Minerva[63]. So that, you see, there is nothing consistent in all this, nothing determinate, nothing upon which the mind can rest with even a probability of truth[64]."

147 '*You* may interpret the connexion of Jupiter

Noachian Flood, if we may believe Eusebius. And as these were called by the Latins *Dii Penates*, which Macrobius [Saturnalia, Lib. iii. cap. 4, § 6. ed. *Janus*], thus interprets, *Dii per quos penitus spiramus, per quos habemus corpus, per quos rationem animi possidemus*, that is, The Gods, by whom we live, and move, and have our being; but Varro in Arnobius [*l. c.*] *Dii qui sunt intrinsecus, atque in intimis penetralibus cœli*, 'the Gods, who are in the most inward recesses of heaven;' so were they called by the Samothracians Κάβειροι or *Cabiri*, that is, as Varro rightly interprets the word, θεοὶ δυνατοί, or *Divi Potes*, the powerful and mighty Gods. Which *Cabiri* being plainly the Hebrew כבודים gives just occasion to suspect, that this ancient tradition of three divine hypostases (unquestionably entertained by Orpheus, Pythagoras, and Plato amongst the Greeks, and probably by the Egyptians and Persians) sprung originally from the Hebrews.'

with Ceres, to signify rain gliding into the bosom of the earth. *Another* may give it a more plausible meaning: a third may assign a different one; and each particular thing may receive an infinite number of interpretations, according to the different geniuses and dispositions of the interpreters. For as the supposition of an allegory is adopted in obscure cases, and there is no certain and determinate end to which the meaning is necessarily directed, every man is at equal liberty to strain it to his own opinion. How then can you extract certainties from ambiguities, and affix one signification to a story, which admits of innumerable expositions[65]?' Again, 'Why do you select particular stories, or parts of stories? If they be all allegory, give the interpretation of each particular. If they be partly allegorical, and partly literal, by what rule or art do you distinguish one from the other[66]?'

'Your interpretations are directly opposite to

[65] Vos Jovis et Cereris coitum imbrem dicitis dictum telluris in gremium lapsum: potest alius aliud et argutius fingere et veri cum similitudine suspicari, potest aliud tertius, potest aliud quartus atque ut se tulerint ingeniorum opinantium qualitates, ita singulæ res possunt infinitis interpretationibus explicari. Cum enim rebus ab occlusis omnis ista quæ dicitur allegoria sumatur, nec habeat finem certum, in quo re quæ dicitur sit fixa atque immota sententia, uni cuique liberum est in id quod velit attrahere lectionem et affirmare id positum, in quod eum sua suspicio et conjectura opinabilis duxerit. Quod cum ita se habeat, qui potestis res certas rebus ab dubiis sumere, atque unam adjungere significationem dicto, quod per modos videatis innumeros expositionum varietate deduci? Arnobius *adv. Nat.* Lib. v. cap. 34.]

[66] Eligitis quædam vestræ convenientia voluntati, et ex ipsis obtineri contenditis nostras atque adulteras lectiones interiori esse superpositas veritati. Quod tamen ut vobis ita

ancient usage. Allegories were formerly adopted in order to clothe mean and impure things in a comely dress, and to invest them with a dignity which did not naturally belong to them. But, according to your expositions, the most august and chaste things are recorded in most obscene language. Why were not things stated in literal terms? Was there no danger in making gods adulterers? If the shade of allegorical obscurity had not involved the subject, the truth would have been obvious to the learner, and the dignity of the gods would have been preserved inviolate[67].'

The most eminent of the Greek fathers of the third century was Origen. He was educated at Alexandria, and one of his name was a scholar of Ammonius. Whether it was he, or a Pagan philosopher, is not quite so certain. He was a man of great industry, genius, and learning. But his judgment was not always able to moderate the

sese habere, quemadmodum dicitis, annuamus qui scitis aut unde cognoscitis, utra pars sit sententiæ historiæ scripta simplicibus, utra vero sit dissonis atque alienis significationibus tecta. *Ibid.* cap. 36.]

[[67] Antea mos fuit in allegorica dictione honestissimis sensibus obumbrare res turpes et fœdas prolatu honestorum convestirier dignitate. At vero vobis auctoribus per turpitudinem dicuntur res graves et castitate pollentia obscenis commemorantur in vocibus, ut quod olim pravitas veterum verecundia contegebatur, nunc verniliter turpiterque dicatur, dignorum elocutione mutata. Quid prohibet, quid obstabat suis unamquamque vorbis et suis significationibus promere.—An deos adulteros dicere periculum habuit nullum?—Quod si allegoricæ cæcitatis obumbratio tolleretur et facilis ad discendum res esset et deorum dignitas conservaretur illæsa. Arnob. *adv. Nat.* Lib. v. cap. 41.]

fervor of his imagination. He was a warm admirer of Philo, and adopted without reserve the allegorical mode of interpreting Scripture, which an injudicious use of his principles in the second century had introduced into the church of Christ.

[Opp.Tom. IV. p. 19 B, ed. Bened.]
Like the Valentinians, he maintained, that ἀρχή, 'beginning,' indicated a person; and discoursing upon the first chapter of St John's Gospel, he says, that it may signify the supreme Being. Thus: 'The word was in the beginning will signify, that it was in God the Father[68].' Christ is also the beginning, being the wisdom of God, and 'the beginning of his ways:' *Proverbs* viii. 22. Thus, commenting upon the first verse in the book of *Genesis*,

Hom. in Gen. c. 1. p. 1.
[Opp. Tom. II. p. 52 c, ed. Bened.]

'In the beginning God created the heaven and the earth,' he says, What is the beginning of all things but our Lord and Saviour Christ Jesus, the first-begotten of every creature? In this beginning therefore, that is, in his word or reason, God made the heaven and the earth. Like Plotinus, he says, the Father is in all respects one and simple; but our Saviour is many[69], on account of the variety of his names and relations, as being the way, the truth, and the life; as being wisdom and righteousness, and sanctification, and redemption—αὐτοαλήθεια, the 'prototype of the truth,' which is in

[68] Οὐκ ἀτόπως δὲ καὶ τὸν τῶν ὅλων θεὸν ἐρεῖ τις ἀρχήν, σαφῶς προπίπτων ὅτι ἀρχὴ υἱοῦ ὁ πατήρ—ἐν ἀρχῇ ἦν ὁ λόγος, λόγον νοῶν τὸν υἱὸν παρὰ τὸ εἶναι ἐν τῷ πατρὶ λεγόμενον εἶναι ἐν ἀρχῇ, p. 17.

[69] Ὁ Θεὸς μὲν οὖν πάντῃ ἕν ἐστι καὶ ἁπλοῦν. ὁ δὲ σωτὴρ ἡμῶν —πολλὰ γίγνεται, p. 19, [*Opp.* Tom. IV. p. 21 D.]

[70] Ἀσώματον ὑπόστασιν ποικίλων θεωρημάτων, περιεχόντων τοὺς τῶν ὅλων λόγους, ζῶσαν καὶ οἱονεὶ ἔμψυχον. *Comm. in Johann.* p. 36, [*Opp.* Tom. IV. p. 39 E.]

reasonable souls, p. 99.—αὐτοδικαιοσύνη ἡ οὐσιώδης, [Opp.Tom. IV. p. 107 c.]
'substantial righteousness,' p. 100.—proceeding from [Ibid. p. 108 A.]
the Father, as will does from mind. He terms him
the living, and, as it were, animated incorporeal
substance of various theorems, containing the reasons of all things[70]. He distinguishes the divine
intellect or wisdom from the *logos*, though he assigns them both to Christ. For the Scriptures so
explicitly declare the *logos*, to which they attribute
the Creation, to have been Christ, the second person; that he could not, as Plotinus did, assign it an
hypostasis distinct from intellect, and denominate
it the third person in the divine nature. Having
quoted *Psalm* xlv. 1, he says, the heart signifies the
intellectual power of God; the *logos* that power
which declares the things contained in it[71]; and he
says, that the *logos* always was in wisdom.

In explaining the derivation of the third person
of the Holy Trinity, he approaches very near the
doctrine of Plotinus. 'The Holy Ghost,' says he,
'seems to stand in need of the Son, who administers to his subsistence, not only that he might *be*,
but also that he might be wise, and reasonable, and
just, and whatever else we ought to understand him
to be, by a participation of the forementioned conceptions of Christ[72]. And I think, that the Holy

[71] Τὴν καρδίαν τοῦ Θεοῦ τὴν νοητικὴν αὐτοῦ καὶ προθετικὴν περὶ τῶν ὅλων δύναμιν ἐκληπτέον, τὸν δὲ λόγον τῶν ἐν ἐκείνῃ ἐπαγγελτικόν [l. ἀπαγγελτικόν], p. 42, [*Opp.* Tom. IV. p. 45 E.]

[72] Μόνου τοῦ μονογενοῦς φύσει υἱοῦ ἀρχῆθεν τυγχάνοντος, οὗ χρῄζειν ἔοικε τὸ ἅγιον πνεῦμα, διακονοῦντος αὐτοῦ τῇ ὑποστάσει, οὐ μόνον εἰς τὸ εἶναι, ἀλλὰ καὶ σόφον εἶναι, καὶ λογικὸν, καὶ δίκαιον, καὶ πᾶν ὁτιποτοῦν χρὴ αὐτὸ νοεῖν τυγχάνειν, κατὰ μετόχην τῶν προειρημένων ἡμῖν Χριστοῦ ἐπινοιῶν κ.τ.λ., p. 57, [*Ibid.* p. 61 c.]

Spirit communicates the matter, if I may so call it, of the gifts from God to those, who are sanctified by him and the participation of him, the said matter of the gifts being wrought by God, administered by Christ, and sustained by the Holy Spirit.'

This likewise bears some resemblance to what Philo says of the divine powers; principles, which Origen, unawed by the example of Praxeas and the Patripassians, whose heresy probably sprung from them, has in other places expressly applied to the second and third persons of the blessed Trinity. In his first *Homily* on Isaiah, he says, that the two seraphim who stood round the throne were our Lord Jesus and the Holy Spirit. He quotes the authority of Philo for this interpretation in both the third chapter of the first book, and in the second chapter of the fourth book, of his treatise περὶ ἀρχῶν.

It is not easy to ascertain exactly the precise opinions of so fanciful an interpreter and so loose a reasoner as Origen. But this, I think, we may venture to affirm, that they were not so exceptionable as the principles and reasonings which he advanced in the defence and explanation of them. His principles and reasonings contain in them the seeds of many heresies; but he often protests

margin notes:
p. 624. [Opp. Tom. III. p. 107 B.]
p. 757. [Tom. I. p. 61.]
p. 843. [Tom. I. p. 189 B.]
152

⁷³ Λόγον οἷον τὸν ἐκ καρδίας ἀνθρώπου νομίζουσι τὸν τοῦ Θεοῦ, καὶ σοφίαν ὁποίαν τὴν ἐν ψυχῇ, καὶ διὰ τοῦτο πρόσωπον ἓν τὸν Θεὸν ἅμα τῷ λόγῳ φασίν· ὥσπερ καὶ τὸν ἄνθρωπον ἅμα τῷ ἑαυτοῦ λόγῳ ἄνθρωπον ἕνα. Athanasius *contra Sab. Greg.* p. 651, [*Opp.* Tom. I. p. 37 E.]

⁷⁴ Οὐδὲ ὡς τοῦ ἑνὸς δὶς ὀνομαζομένου, ὥστε τὸν αὐτὸν ἀλλότε μὲν πατέρα, ἀλλότε δὲ υἱὸν ἑαυτοῦ γίγνεσθαι· τοῦτο γὰρ Σαβέλλιος

against those heretical applications of them, and advances, in opposition, sound doctrines.

The most important heresy which sprung up in the third century was that of Sabellius, whether we consider it in itself or in its consequences. He adopted the usual method of explaining the nature of the Son by stating him to be the wisdom or the reason of the Father. But he maintained that the reason of God was identically the same with God, constituting one person with the Father; in the same manner as a man together with his reason composes one man[73]. Thus the same person, being really one but having two names, is at one time the father, and at another time his own son[74].

This opinion of Sabellius was embraced by some bishops of Pentapolis in Upper Libya; insomuch that scarcely any other doctrine relative to the son of God was taught in the churches of those parts[75]. Dionysius, bishop of Alexandria, to whom the care of those churches belonged, sent and counselled those who had been guilty, to relinquish that impious doctrine, and return to the true faith. When he found that his expostulations had not produced the intended effect, he wrote them a letter in which he undertook to prove the falsehood of the doctrine which they were so strenuous in

φρονήσας αἱρετικὸς ἐκρίθη. Athan. contra Arian. Orat. IV. p. 456, [Orat. III. § 4, Opp. Tom. I. p. 553.] Τὸ ἐν διώνυμον, Σαβελλίου τὸ ἐπιτήδευμα, τὸν αὐτὸν υἱὸν καὶ πατέρα λέγοντος. Ibid. v. p. 525, [Orat. III. § 9.]

[75] Ἐν Πενταπόλει τῆς ἄνω Λιβύης τηνικαῦτά τινες τῶν ἐπισκόπων ἐφρόνησαν τὰ Σαβελλίου· καὶ τοσοῦτον ἴσχυσαν ταῖς ἐπινοίαις, ὡς ὀλίγου δεῖν μηκέτι ἐν ταῖς ἐκκλησίαις κηρύττεσθαι τὸν υἱὸν τοῦ Θεοῦ. Athan. De Sent. Dion. contra Arian. p. 552, [§ 5, Tom. I. p. 246 D.]

propagating. In this letter, while he was perhaps too earnestly insisting upon the difference between the Father and the Son, he made use of reasonings and expressions, which seemed to some men to entrench too much upon the dignity of the second person of the Holy Trinity. However, when he was accused, he extricated himself from the difficulty either by retracting his error, or by explaining away the seemingly offensive passages in his letter, and by solemn professions of a true faith. Athanasius defends him by comparing his conduct to that of a skilful physician, who, when he is called in to a patient, considers only the nature of the disorder under which he labours, and administers such remedies for the removal of it, as if applied without any reference to a case of that particular 154 description, might have a tendency to produce a malady of a directly opposite nature.

Whatever ground there was for these insinuations to his prejudice, it is certain that in the ensuing century the followers of Arius endeavoured to shelter themselves under the authority of the name of Dionysius. Athanasius, who carefully watched every movement of the Arians, did not suffer them long to enjoy this advantage without molestation. He composed an elaborate treatise, in order to vindicate his venerable predecessor from the imputation of favouring those opinions, for the suppression of which he himself was exerting all the powers of a vigorous mind and an ardent spirit.

Arius was a Presbyter at Alexandria; and the heresy that goes by his name, and which occasioned so much confusion in the church in the fourth century, either originated from or gave rise to a violent contest between him and Alexander, the bishop of Alexandria. Arius explained and defended his principles in a treatise, which he denominated *Thalia*. But as neither that work nor any writings of his opponent, Alexander, are extant; all the knowledge that we can have of their respective principles, must be derived from the writings of others. Athanasius, who succeeded Alexander in the see of Alexandria, and was considered from the first as the strongest bulwark of the cause, may be safely deemed to have given a just representation of the principles of his own party. And as he entered into the controversy more deeply than any other; it is from him that we have the best chance of collecting the principles of Arius.

I wish it to be observed that I am now enquiring not about the respective doctrines of the contending parties, (for these are notorious,) but about the principles which led to those doctrines and the modes of explaining them. Arius accused Alexander of professing the doctrine of Sabellius, who confounded the persons of the Father and the Son. Alexander accused Arius of degrading the Son to the rank of a creature.

In order to understand clearly this controversy, it will be proper to call to mind the sophisticated doctrines of Philo, which were composed of heterogeneous principles, derived from the books of the Old Testament and the writings of Plato. These doctrines were still further distorted by the early writers of the Christian Church, and rashly applied to explain the sublime mysteries of our holy religion. The word Λόγος is used by Philo in three distinct senses, in each of which it has been applied by Christian writers to the second person of the Holy Trinity. He denominates by it, first, the divine intellect; secondly, the conception of that intellect, the idea or system of ideas which is the production of its reflex act, and the internal object of its contemplation; thirdly, the external expression of that conception. Thus, when he is speaking of the intelligible world, of that plan or pattern which the Deity formed before he created the external world; he says, it is not allowable to say that it is in any place. For as the plan that an architect forms of a city which he is about to build, is not in any place, but in the soul of the artist; in the same manner the world of ideas can have no other place but the divine intellect which arranged those things[76]. Farther on he says, if a man would use plain words he would say, that the intelligible world is nothing else but the reasoning of God, while he was in the act of making the world[77]. The use of the word in the third sense is too common for it to be necessary that I should quote any passages to prove it.

[76] Τὸν αὐτὸν τρόπον οὐδ᾽ ὁ ἐκ τῶν ἰδέων κόσμος ἄλλον ἂν ἔχοι τόπον, ἢ τὸν θεῖον λόγον τὸν ταῦτα διακοσμήσαντα. Περὶ Κοσμοπ. p. 4.

[77] Εἰ δέ τις ἐθελήσειε γυμνοτέροις χρήσασθαι τοῖς ὀνόμασιν, οὐδὲν ἂν ἕτερον εἴποι τὸν νοητὸν εἶναι κόσμον, ἢ Θεοῦ λόγον ἤδη κοσμοποιοῦντος, p. 5.

I have already produced instances, in which the early fathers applied the term in these several significations to Christ. If the principles of Alexander were the same as those which were advanced by Athanasius; he applied the word Λόγος to the second person of the Holy Trinity in the first sense only. When he is disputing with the Arians about the eternity of the second person, he, with an air of triumph, bids them add this to their question, Whether there ever was a time when the essentially existent God was destitute of reason or intellect[78]. But in his exposition of faith, in order to make his meaning clearly and accurately understood upon so important a subject, he asserts this doctrine with all imaginable caution, to the absolute exclusion of the explanations of Arius, Sabellius, and other heretics[79]. He said, that the error of the Sabellians arose from their false notions of this reason or wisdom and word of God, which constitutes the second person of the Holy Trinity. They conceived of God as of man, and supposed that the Word of God was similar to that which issues from the heart of man; and that the wisdom of God was such as that which is in the soul of man. On this account they say that God together with his word consti-

[78] Ὁ ὢν Θεὸς ἦν ποτε ἄλογος; *Cont. Arian. Orat.* II. p. 330, [I. p. 421, § 24, *ed. B.*]

[79] Εἰς ἕνα μονογενῆ λόγον, σοφίαν, υἱόν, ἐκ τοῦ πατρὸς ἀνάρχως καὶ ἀϊδίως γεγεννημένον. λόγον δὲ οὐ προφορικὸν, οὐκ ἐνδιάθετον, οὐκ ἀπορροίαν τοῦ τελείου, οὐ τμῆσιν τῆς ἀπαθοῦς φύσεως, οὔτε προβολὴν, ἀλλ᾽ υἱὸν αὐτοτελῆ, ζῶντά τε καὶ ἐνεργοῦντα. κ.τ.λ. *Expos. Fidei*, p. 240, [Tom. I. p. 99, *ed. B.*]

tutes but one person; in the same manner as a man together with his word or reason composes but one man. *Cont. Sab. Greg.* p. 651. Upon this he remarks that the word of a man neither lives nor subsists, and is only the motion of a living and subsisting heart; and passes away as soon as it is uttered. But the word of the Lord, as the Psalmist declares, endureth for ever in heaven. This he elsewhere calls substantial word and substantial wisdom[80].

Arius maintained, on the contrary, that this principle which stated the real wisdom and reason of God to be the Son in the Holy Trinity, is mere Sabellianism. When he denied the eternity of the Son, he did not affirm that there ever was a time when God was without wisdom or reason. He has in himself his own wisdom and his own reason, which is not Christ, but in which he made Christ[81].

There are some passages in the writings of Athanasius, which seem to intimate that the principles of Arius were connected with some Jewish and Grecian tenets. He says, that impiety is introduced by their principles, or rather Judaism, different from that contained in the Scriptures, which has Hellenism closely following it[82]. In another

---

[80] Οὐσιώδης λόγος καὶ οὐσιώδης σοφία. *Contr. Arian. Orat.* v. p. 520, [IV. § 1, p. 618 A, ed. Ben.]

[81] Σόφος μέν ἐστι καὶ οὐκ ἄλογος, ἰδίαν δὲ ἔχει ἐν ἑαυτῷ σοφίαν καὶ ἴδιον λόγον, οὐ τὸν Χριστὸν δὲ, ἀλλ' ἐν ᾧ καὶ τὸν Χριστὸν ἐποίησε. *Orat.* v. *Contra Arian.* p. 522, [*Or.* IV. p. 620 B.] See to the same purpose the third oration, p. 408, [*Or.* II. p. 487, sq.]

[82] Ἀθεότης γὰρ ἐκ τούτων εἰσάγεται, καὶ μᾶλλον παρὰ τὰς γρα-

passage he exhibits a more particular account of the principles of Arius. By comparing that with a passage of the same import near the beginning of Philo περὶ κοσμοποιΐας, it will be obvious from what source Arius, as well as Tertullian, derived his notions. God, says he, was alone, and reason and wisdom were not yet. But when he was disposed to create us, he then made one being, and named him reason, and son, and wisdom, that by means of him he might create us. There are then, says he, two wisdoms; one God's own, and subsisting with him. In this wisdom the other, the son, was formed[83]. In this passage we have the strongest features of the twofold *logos* of Philo ; viz. The intelligible world, which he calls also the reasoning of God when he was in the act of creating the world, the pattern according to which this sensible world was made : and secondly, The wisdom and intellect of God, in which that pattern, the intelligible world, was formed. Athanasius in a great number of places controverts the principle of Arius, that the son was produced on our account, and for the express purpose of forwarding our creation; and that he is called the wisdom of God in a figurative sense, on account of the great display, which

φὰς Ἰουδαϊσμὸς, ἔχων ἐγγὺς ἐπακολουθοῦντα τὸν Ἑλληνισμόν, p. 296, [*Epist. ad Episc. Æg.* Opp. Tom. I. p. 283 B, *ed. B.*]

[83] Ἦν γάρ, φησι, μόνος ὁ Θεὸς, καὶ οὔπω ἦν ὁ λόγος καὶ ἡ σοφία· εἶτα θελήσας ἡμᾶς δημιουργῆσαι, τότε δὲ [δὴ *l. B.*] πεποίηκεν ἕνα τινὰ, καὶ ὠνόμασεν αὐτὸν λόγον καὶ υἱὸν καὶ σοφίαν, ἵνα ἡμᾶς δι᾽ αὐτοῦ δημιουργήσῃ· δύο γοῦν σοφίας φησὶν εἶναι, μίαν μὲν, τὴν ἰδίαν καὶ συνυπάρχουσαν τῷ Θεῷ, τὸν δὲ υἱὸν ἐν αὐτῇ [ταύτῃ *l. B.*] τῇ σοφίᾳ γεγενῆσθαι. *Orat.* II. pp. 310, 11, [*Or.* I. p. 409 B, C.]

his nature exhibits, of the divine wisdom in which he was formed.

These modes of explanation and defence were now so thoroughly established, and from this time assumed so regular a form, that it is unnecessary to pursue the subject farther.

CONCLUSION.

THE inferences which I would draw from the preceding investigation are two : first, That a Trinity of Persons in the divine nature was the genuine and peculiar doctrine of the primitive Christian Church. Secondly, That it is extremely dangerous to affect to be wise in holy things above what is written in the word of God.

I. How much soever the early writers of the Church differ in their method of explaining the *nature* of the three divine persons, and their *relation* to each other; they are in a manner unanimous in their profession of the general doctrine. The great and important question seems to be, From whence did they derive this opinion? Most of the defenders and opposers of this doctrine in modern times agree in maintaining that the doctrine of the Trinity is delivered and inculcated in the writings of Plato. Hence the orthodox conclude, that, though this great mystery is more fully set forth in the Holy Scriptures, and derives its chief authority from divine revelation; yet, either the doctrine itself is congenial to the mind of man, and regularly deducible from principles of reason; or, that it was handed down in the heathen world by uninterrupted tradition from remote antiquity. The opposers of our faith, on the contrary, infer from the same premises, that the doctrine itself is no part of genuine Christianity: that it is the natural production of philosophy, falsely so called: and that it was introduced into the Church of Christ by men, who with their subtleties distorted the graceful form, and corrupted the simplicity of our holy religion.

In the course of the preceding enquiry, I have found myself obliged to differ in some points from both those parties. After a minute and impartial examination of the writings of Plato, I cannot find anything which sufficiently proves him to have had even an obscure knowledge of the mysterious doctrine of the Trinity. None of his immediate followers taught it: none of his personal enemies or philosophical rivals urged it as an objection against him: none of the sects which branched off from the academy professed it. When the arts and learning of Greece were imported into Italy: when poets, philosophers, and statesmen considered it as the most noble employment

[Horat. II. Epist. ii.v.45.]

inter sylvas Academi quærere verum:

when Plato was esteemed to have spoken as it were the language of the gods; and all the ingenuity and eloquence of Rome were exerted to unfold his principles, and recommend his conclusions—during this long and enlightened period, no traces are to be found in the works of heathen writers of this profound, this peculiar doctrine.

The discovery was not made till philosophers became Christians, and Christians became philosophers. The converted philosopher endeavoured to shew to his unconverted brethren the superior brilliancy of the light which he enjoyed as a Christian. To this purpose he contended that Christianity was not without his evidences even among themselves: that intimations of the sublime doctrines of revelation were to be found in the writings of the philosophers of Greece: that those sages to whom they looked up with so much reverence had nothing whereof to glory: that they were mere retailers of scraps and fragments from holy writ, mutilated by their ignorance, and obscured by their speculations.

The conceit was captivating: it was seized with avidity. The Apologist urged the Pagan to approach the pure fountain of God's word, and not to drink of the muddy stream of human speculation. The Christian teacher, while he traced out fanciful resemblances, conveyed to his hearers a great idea of the extent of his knowledge and the subtilty of his wit.

If the expedient tended at all to promote the progress of Christianity; it did so for a very short time. Error is multiform, and its cause may be advanced in ten thousand different ways. But nothing that is not entirely founded on fact, and perfectly conformable to the nature of things, can coalesce with the simple texture of truth, or accord with the symmetry of its parts. The unnatural conjunction will inevitably, sooner or later, weaken the good cause which it was intended to support. It is, to use the words of the prophet Isaiah, 'a staff of a broken reed, whereon if a man lean, it will go into his hand and pierce it.' So are false conceits to all that trust in them. The battery was soon turned against Christianity by the sophists of those times.

The author of our holy profession disclaimed all compromise and communication with the several religions of the heathen world, which he represented to lie in darkness and the shadow of death. He was a light to lighten the Gentiles, and rose with healing on his wings. He told his followers, that no one knew the Father but the Son, and he to whom the Son should reveal him. He unfolded such mysteries concerning the divine nature and proceedings, as even the angels of God had before desired in vain to look into.

The disputers of this world soon saw the advantage which the indiscreet preachers of our holy religion gave them against the high claims of their master and his immediate followers; and they availed themselves of it to the utmost extent. They readily admitted the supposed fact, that the doctrines contained in the writings of Plato, and those propounded in the Gospel, were essentially the same. But the conclusion which they drew from this common principle was widely different from that which was held forth by the Christians. They denied that the Holy Scriptures were the original fountain of all wisdom. They maintained, on the contrary, that the founders of the different sects of Grecian philosophy and popular mythology, more especially Plato, derived their information from the same source as the author of Christianity, which was no other than the genuine dictates of reason and nature. Where then, they triumphantly asked, is the superiority for which you contend over all the nations of the earth? Why do you call upon us to relinquish the wise and venerable systems and institutions of our ancestors, when you have nothing essentially different to offer us in their stead?

The sophists of those times satisfied themselves with the positions, that the characteristic doctrines of Christianity were really, though obscurely, taught in the writings of Plato; and that they were concealed under allegories in the fables of popular mythology. The state of religion and philosophy did not admit of the possibility of their going farther than this point at that time. It was reserved for the disputers of later ages to assert, that those profound doctrines are in truth no part of genuine Christianity: that they were the subtil inventions of men: and that they were originally introduced into Christianity from the writings of Plato. As this assertion has been frequently repeated, though without the shadow of a proof, it deserved a minute enquiry.

In assertions of this kind some particular time or person must be pointed out, in order to give a kind of plausibility to the thing asserted. Justin Martyr has been almost unavoidably fixed upon in the instance before us. To have carried up the general corruption much nearer to the time of the apostles would have been scarcely consistent with probability. To have brought it down lower would have been impossible, as the doctrine of the Trinity is manifestly asserted in the works of that Apologist. He was, moreover, familiarly conversant with the principles of Plato and other Grecian philosophers before he embraced Christianity; and he was particularly fond of proving to his unconverted brethren, the superior advantages which he derived from the study of the Holy Scriptures, in consequence of the originality, the purity, and the extent of the discoveries relating to divine things that were contained in them.

If Justin derived his opinion of a Trinity of Persons in the divine nature from the writings of Plato, and from thence transplanted them into Christianity; either he adopted the received notions of the Platonists of his own or preceding times; or by his sagacity he had discovered in the writings of Plato some doctrines, which had escaped the scrutiny and penetration of all others. That Justin by his sagacity discovered what had eluded the diligent search of the long list of sages of Greece and Rome, who flourished between the days of Plato and the second century of the Christian æra, is, I conceive, what our opponents will not be very forward to advance, or even admit. If they affirm, that the followers of Plato had actually discovered that doctrine in his writings, and had openly and explicitly avowed it in or before the days of Justin, it rests upon them to prove it. As far as my researches have extended, I have not been able to find any one instance, in

which the doctrine had been maintained by Pagan
philosophers[1], in the same plain and decided manner, as by the Fathers of the Christian Church. By these it was propounded as the criterion of their orthodoxy, as the ground-work of their faith. But the cultivators of human wisdom appear to have been total strangers to it; till it was disclosed to them by a teacher of philosophy, who had been educated in the bosom of Christianity. Then, and not till then, they used it, as a key

[1] The high estimation, in which Lord Montboddo and Dr Heberden are deservedly held by the learned world, obliges me to take notice of the following note in that noble lord's *Treatise on the Origin and Progress of Language*, Book II. cap. 2, p. 339: "A learned and worthy gentleman of my acquaintance in London, Dr Heberden, shewed me a passage in Seneca's *Consolatio ad Helviam*, from which it appears, that it, (the doctrine of the Trinity) was known to the Stoics. His words are, speaking of the misfortune that had befallen this woman: Id actum est, mihi crede, ab illo, quisquis formator universi fuit, sive ille Deus est potens omnium, sive incorporalis ratio, ingentium operum artifex, sive divinus spiritus, per omnia maxima et minima æquali intentione diffusus, sive fatum et immutabilis causarum inter se cohærentium series." Senecæ *Consol. ad Helviam*, cap. 8. To my mind this passage does not appear to have the least tendency towards proving the point, in support of which it is cited. I should as soon undertake to prove, that Pope inculcated the doctrine of the Trinity, from the last line of the first stanza in his Universal Prayer:

<blockquote>
Father of all! in ev'ry age,
In ev'ry clime ador'd,
By saint, by savage, and by sage,
Jehovah, Jove, or Lord!
</blockquote>

The poet asserts, that the first cause is worshipped by men in all states, however they may differ about the name, by which they address him. In like manner the philosopher refers the calamity to the appointment of the supreme Being, however he may have been characterized by philosophers, and by whatever appellation he is to be distinguished.

to unlock the abstract subtilties of Plato, and to throw a decent veil over the extravagant and licentious fables of Pagan mythology.

Again, the manner in which Plotinus conducts his argumentation, is an object deserving our attention. The Christian opened the sacred volume; and, as he read, he found, or believed that he found, the profound doctrine of the Trinity of Persons in the Godhead revealed in it. The truth of the doctrine he rested upon the authority of Holy Writ. For an explanation of the nature of those beings whom it concerns, and of the relation which they bear to each other, where his heavenly guide was silent, he had recourse to the subtilties of human wit. This was the natural course for those to take who derived their information from another, and rested the truth of their tenets upon the authority of their teacher.

But this was not the course which Plotinus followed. His object was not to prove the truth of the doctrine by the authority of Plato, but to bend the language of Plato to a consistency with the doctrine. He does not even profess to have learned it from that great master of philosophy; but undertakes to deduce it by general reasoning from abstract notions of entity, mind, and soul. Having thus drawn his conclusions, he next applies them in illustration of the doctrines of Plato.

This, I conceive, is the exact course which a man would pursue, who had derived the doctrine from another source, and wished to prove, that it was also to be found in the writings of Plato. I ask,

Would any one, but a man thus circumstanced, have discovered this profound doctrine in the story of the birth of Venus, or in the mythological fable of Cronus, Rhea, and Jupiter?

I will not dwell upon the inconsistencies that frequently occur in the explanations, which are given by the advocates for the Platonic Trinity. They are obliged by their system to make the mythological Ζεῦς sometimes the first, sometimes the second, and sometimes the third hypostasis. And, in their interpretations of Plato, they sometimes make δημιουργὸς the first, νοῦς the second, and ψυχὴ the third hypostasis: at other times they make δημιουργὸς, at other times ἰδέα ἡ παράδειγμα, at other times ψυχὴ the second hypostasis.

II. The second inference which I would make from the preceding investigation is, that it is extremely dangerous to affect to be wise in holy things, above what is written in the word of GOD. It is to this disposition, I conceive, that we are to attribute, in a great measure, the present miserable condition of the Jewish nation. They would not be satisfied with that degree of information which Jehovah condescended to give them of the order of his dispensations, and of the nature of that being, who was to come from GOD as their Saviour and their King. They rashly speculated upon things that were not revealed, and they framed to themselves a system of belief widely different from the truth. Hence, when in the fulness of time GOD sent his Son into the world, the world knew him not: when he came unto his own, his own received him not.

The same spirit of curiosity and desire of prying into heavenly things have, though in a different manner, produced very pernicious consequences in the Church of Christ.

The writings of Philo Judæus furnished the Fathers of the Christian Church with the fatal means of deceiving themselves and others. The figurative language in which that author delivered himself concerning the Logos, whenever he meant by it either the divine intellect, its internal operation, the ideal object of its contemplation, or the external expression of it, led them to imagine that he attributed to it a real and essential personality. From the epithets affixed to this supposed person, they naturally conceived that he could be no other than our Lord and Saviour, Jesus Christ. To make this plausible they maintained, that what was expressed by the word Logos, was not in God, as it was in man, a mere power, or operation, or notion, or word; but was a real and living substance, possessed of a personality distinct from the great principle of existence, to which it belonged. This received countenance from the doctrines of Plato, that ideas were most properly the real entities.

Hence was devised the metaphysical argument for the eternity of the second person of the Trinity, which was built upon this plain and incontrovertible maxim, that God the Father could never have been destitute of reason. Hence the second person is called by Athanasius substantial *Logos* and substantial Wisdom. Hence arose the conceit, that he flowed necessarily from the divine intellect exerted on itself. Hence Origen styles him, The living and, as it were, animated substance of various theorems, containing the reasons of all things.

It unfortunately happened, that many signal heresies were produced by men's accepting a false hypothesis and an erroneous explanation, and turning them against the doctrine, for the illustration of which they were devised.—The Gnostics, presuming that every production of the divine intellect was necessarily a substance, imagined an almost infinite number of such productions, and attempted to explain by them the origin of those several orders of Æons, which constituted so striking a part of the eastern philosophy.

173 Praxeas and Sabellius admitted that Christ was the intellect and wisdom of God the Father, and thence concluded, that he was one with him, as well in personality as in essence; thus attempting to subvert a doctrine by means of an hypothesis, which was founded, if it had any foundation at all, upon the supposed truth of that doctrine, and which was advanced, not to prove, but to explain it.

Arius seems to have felt the force of the reasoning of Praxeas and Sabellius; but he was too well versed in the Scriptures not to see, that a distinct personality is in them attributed to Christ. He therefore perceived the necessity of projecting a new mode of defence; but, like many others, who had gone before him, he embraced hypothetical explanations, to the injury of the truth, which was to be explained. He acknowledged with Praxeas and Sabellius, that the real intellect or wisdom of God was no other than God himself. He admitted with Tertullian, that the immediate production of the divine intellect was necessarily a living substance. Hence he maintained, that Christ was, what Philo called the intelligible world; or, as Origen styled him, the living and animated substance of various theorems, containing the reasons of all things; denominated Logos, and Son, and Wisdom, though not the real wisdom of God, yet formed in it; not existing from all eternity, but created on our account, that God by means of him might create us[2].

Thus it appears that, though Christians did not, as has been maintained by some, derive the great and characteristic doctrines of their holy profession from the impure source of Pagan philosophy; they did, at a very early period indeed, adopt principles and modes of interpretation, which but ill accorded with the simplicity of the Gospel. They presumed to intrude with unhallowed step into the sanctuary of the most High, and to attempt with sacrilegious hands to tear off the veil from

---

[2] So strongly was this hypothesis rooted in the minds of men, that it was not even yet abandoned; and Arius has been combated on his own ground. It has been admitted, that Christ was the intelligible world, containing the ideas of all things. Yet still his proper eternity has been maintained upon metaphysical principles. The divine intellect is from its own nature ever active. Before all external creation it was employed from

those august mysteries, which God himself had concealed from human sight. The event was such as might naturally have been expected. Professing themselves to be wise, they became fools; and God gave many of them up unto a reprobate mind. 175 All the extravagancies and impurities of the several orders of Gnostics, all the impiety of Praxeas and Sabellius, the heresy of Arius, and the bloody contentions, which rent in sunder the Eastern Church, and paved the way for the reception of the impostures of Mahomet, are to be referred to this source. Hence also have arisen many of those disputes and bitter reproaches, which in latter days have disgraced the Christian name, and injured the cause of genuine piety. Hence was derived the most opprobrious of all imputations, that the sublime doctrine of the Trinity, the distinguishing feature of Christianity in every age, was drawn from the dregs of Pagan philosophy. This should serve as a warning to men, if any thing can, to confine themselves in their researches within the bounds that have been prescribed to them by divine wisdom, and to satisfy themselves with such communications, as God has thought proper to make, of his nature and dispensations.

If they would act wisely, they should exert

eternity in an internal contemplation of the ideal pattern of the things, which were in due time to be created. The reader may see this argument very ingeniously drawn out and enforced by Norris, in his *Theory of the Ideal* or *Intelligible World;* who, in the true spirit of his system, maintains, that all things were made not *by* Christ, but *according to* Christ, that is, according to those ideas or patterns, which compose his essence.

their faculties, first, in proving the authenticity of revelation; secondly, in ascertaining the genuine sense of it. For they may be well assured that, if God has made to men any revelation of his nature and dispensations, he has revealed as much as is proper for them to know, in their present circumstances. Nay, if they attempt to proceed a step farther than their heavenly guide has condescended to conduct them, they will not only be disappointed in the expectation of making any real progress, but will even be led out of the way, and removed much farther from the object of their vain pursuit, than if they had stopped at the point where divine Providence had set them their bounds, that they should not pass.

Of this every one is sensible, with respect to preceding dispensations. We are all ready to acknowledge, that the intimation with which God favoured Adam, respecting the seed of the woman, was adapted with wonderful wisdom and mercy to his particular situation: that it conveyed the precise degree of information, which the otherwise desperate state of the affairs of our first parent required; but that it was not sufficient to enable him to trace out that amazing scheme of Providence, which the divine Being afterwards vouchsafed in the fulness of time gradually to disclose to the sons of men.—The same observation will apply to every period of the Patriarchal and Jewish dispensations; till God sent his Son into the world in the likeness of sinful flesh, when perhaps as much of the mystery of godliness was revealed, as is requisite to be known by man in this our state of pilgrimage.

As so extraordinary an atonement was made for the transgression of our first parents, and the depravity of their posterity, the display of that stupendous proceeding seems well calculated to produce in men a strong sense of the heinous nature of sin, and a dread and abhorrence of its pollutions. It is the language of religion, that we are to consider this world as a state of discipline, preparatory to a future life of superior excellence and enjoyment; and we have every reason to believe, from the representations of the Holy Scriptures, that Christ will reign at the head of his saints in his kingdom of glory. In this view it is easy to perceive how expedient it was, that we, who are hereafter to be his subjects, should, in this our state of discipline, have some intimation of the dignity of our Lord and Master. But it does not thence follow, that it is either expedient or consistent with the limited nature of our faculties, that the mysteries of the divine nature should be completely unfolded to us; or that we, who cannot fully comprehend the internal constitution of the most common object, which is exposed to our senses, should be encouraged to pry into the deep recesses of that Being, whose goings forth have been of old from everlasting. Error, and many times impiety, must be the consequence of so rash and overweening a conceit of our own abilities. It becomes us rather, and will be found in the end to be most consistent with our true interest, to be satisfied with that portion of light which God himself has imparted to us in his holy word; and not to flatter ourselves that we shall be able to encrease it by a pretended philosophy and vain deceit, after the traditions of men, after the rudiments of the world, and not after Christ— *Hæc fere dicere habui de Natura Deorum, non ut eam tollerem, sed ut intelligeretis, quam esset obscura, et quam difficiles explicatus haberet.* Cic. de Nat. Deor. III. 39.

In a former [3] treatise I undertook to demonstrate, that true philosophy has no tendency to undermine divine revelation, and that a well-grounded philosopher may be a true Christian: that the legitimate object of philosophy, as well as of revelation, is truth: that the pursuit of this object, by a careful attention to and investigation of the appearances and operations of nature, has a direct tendency to enliven and invigorate the intellectual powers; and that the possession of it enlarges the capacity of the mind, and prepares it for the reception and right apprehension of the doctrines of Christianity.—In this I have endeavoured to point out some strikingly-pernicious effects, which have arisen from the rash attempt of men to explain the most profound mysteries of the nature and essence of God, by the vain and groundless conceits of speculative sophists; instead of confining themselves to an investigation of the moral character of the Deity by the united aid of reason

---

[3] The dissertation, to which the honorary prize was adjudged, by Teyler's Theological Society, at Haarlem, in April

and revelation, and of the duties which result from the several relations that he bears to them, of Creator, Preserver, Redeemer, Sanctifier, and Judge.

I find that in thus asserting and illustrating the use and abuse of reason, when applied to religion, I have conformed, without being aware of it at the time, to the opinion of a man, whose comprehensive and penetrating mind has contributed not a little towards advancing true philosophy to that exalted state of dignity, which it at present so justly possesses. I will produce this testimony as the conclusion of the whole.

"By the contemplation of nature to induce and enforce the acknowledgment of God, and to demonstrate his power, providence, and goodness, is an excellent argument, and hath been excellently handled by divers. But on the other side, out of the contemplation of nature, or ground of human knowledges, to induce any verity or persuasion concerning the points of faith, is in my judgment not safe: *Da fidei, quæ fidei sunt.* For the heathen themselves conclude as much in that excellent and divine fable of the golden chain: *That Gods and men were not able to draw Jupiter down to the earth; but, contrariwise, Jupiter was able to draw them up to heaven.*

" So as we ought not to attempt to draw down or submit the mysteries of God to our reason; but, contrariwise, to raise and advance our reason to the divine truth. So as in this part of knowledge,

1785. [The prize-medal, which was presented on the occasion, is now in the University Library.]

touching divine philosophy, I am so far from noting any deficience, as I rather note an excess: whereunto I have digressed, because of the extreme prejudice, which both religion and philosophy have received, and may receive, by being commixed together; as that which undoubtedly will make an heretical religion, and an imaginary and fabulous philosophy." BACON *of the Advancement of Learning.*

THE END.

www.ingramcontent.com/pod-product-compliance
Lightning Source LLC
Chambersburg PA
CBHW050802160426
43192CB00010B/1606